BST

FORM 19

Bread Upon the Waters

Bread Upon the Waters

A History of United States Grain Exports

by

Harry Fornari

AURORA PUBLISHERS INCORPORATED
NASHVILLE/LONDON

To Misa

Table of Contents

Preface

Ever since Neolithic man found sixty or seventy centuries ago that the kernels produced by certain grasses could be used as food, grains have been fundamental to the sustenance of human life. With the dawn of civilization, men learned to sow seeds in order to expand the size and regularity of their grain harvests, and, as the family developed into the tribe, new concepts gradually evolved. Among them were the storage of surplus from a bumper crop and the exchange of grain for other goods. Grain cultivation eventually spread through most of the inhabited globe, but since densities of population increased unevenly in different regions, certain areas became consistent surplus producers of grains while others became chronically dependent on imports of balancing supplies. The basic features of a grain-exporting country, therefore, can be defined as an abundance of fertile land combined with a relatively small population density, advanced agricultural technology, and a well-organized and sophisticated commercial mechanism.

Grain-importing countries, on the other hand, may derive such status from many varying conditions: essentially, where free market conditions prevail, a country will import grain when it has both the need (generally caused by large population density when compared to fertile land) and the ability to purchase (through sufficient foreign exchange or credits); other countries, although poor, may be supplied with grain by surplus producers for strategic or political considerations.

Obviously, there are many factors which differentiate grain exporting from exports of other commodities or manufactured products: exportable quantities are controlled by weather and other natural causes rather than by conscious production decisions alone; grain exports, while of course constituted exclusively of "consumer goods," cannot be put directly into consumption without some form of further processing, and the ultimate products are therefore generally not identifiable as imported merchandise; and since adequate grain supplies can and often do represent the difference between famine and survival for some country's population, grain exporting and importing is often an intrinsic component of national and international policies.

ix

Furthermore, the export marketing arrangements pertaining to the grain trade are far more complex and far-reaching than in almost any other field. The factors affecting supply and demand are particularly diverse and subject to very sudden changes. Among these ever changing factors are weather, blights and plant diseases, genetic developments in seed varieties, changes in modes of transportation and handling. Also important are trends in consumer preference for one kind of grain flour or cereal food over another, and changes in utilization of different types of grain for livestock feeding. Also not to be forgotten are social and political considerations which find expression in direct subsidies to farmers as well as indirect protection through tariffs or other import restrictions on agricultural products grown abroad.

When all is said and done, however, grain exporting is essentially a problem of distribution: distribution in space, through systems for transferring grain supplies from surplus producers to deficit consumers; and distribution in time, through evening out grain supplies from one harvest to the next and from periods of abundance to periods of shortage. In practice, of course, even in a completely free world economy, the vagaries of nature and the foibles of men cause appreciable variations in the solutions of the distribution problems. Basically, though, it is still the law of supply and demand which determines grain prices and consequently, directly or indirectly, types and volumes of production and of domestic consumption as well as exports. When, however, the governments of traditionally importing countries embark on an all-out course of economic protectionism and drastically interfere with the normal flow of grain in world trade channels, the resulting distortion of the normal distribution mechanism is bound to have serious and lasting consequences on the economies of both traditional exporting and traditional importing countries. This was the case in the period following World War II.

The United States, as the largest among the world's grain-exporting countries, is vitally interested in taking any steps necessary to maintain and expand her agricultural exports, the first goal being the lowering and elimination of the trade barriers which hamper such exports. After all, as the Williams Commission pointed out in its report of July, 1971, to President Nixon: "In no sector of the economy are domestic and international policies more closely related than in agriculture. . . . Endowed with plentiful good land and highly efficient technology and organization, we have a productive capacity far in excess of our domestic needs. Only on the basis of large and growing exports can we use our resources efficiently and thereby exploit our comparative advantages in agriculture."

The export of agricultural commodities has always been a vital factor in the American economy, and, even though other products such as cotton or tobacco have dominated the scene from time to time, the mainstay of our farm exports has been and continues to be grain. Knowledge of the past is an admittedly imperfect but nevertheless essential tool in planning for the future, and since an extensive review of the available literature indicates that there is no up-to-date comprehensive history of United States grain exports in existence, in the following pages an attempt is made to supply a concise account of the course of American grain exports from colonial times to the present. It is hoped that such a study, by reviewing the problems encountered and surmounted by the export grain trade in the past, may provide some insight into the problems confronting it now as well as offer some help toward their solution.

Harry Fornari

Great Neck, N. Y.
June, 1972

Acknowledgments

In expressing my gratitude to the many individuals who were kind enough to cooperate and thus contribute in their own way to the completion of this study, I wish to mention first Walter C. Klein, to whom I am deeply indebted for suggesting the project as well as for his continued support and helpful counsel.

Professor James H. Shideler of the University of California at Davis, Editor of *Agricultural History*, Roger Noall, and Carl C. Brasmer, independently read the manuscript making many constructive criticisms and able suggestions: my appreciation for their help is deep and heartfelt.

The manuscript was also reviewed by several of my colleagues: Fred C. Ashner, John P. Muller, Albert Youngman, Warren W. Hecker, A. Henry Becker, George W. Hughes and Gerald J. Mathews. Their observations, based on long and broad experience in the export grain trade, produced a myriad of changes, clarifications, and corrections, for which I thank them collectively and individually. The responsibility for any remaining errors is exclusively mine.

I also wish to thank for their help Dr. Wayne D. Rasmussen, Chief of the Agricultural History Branch of the United States Department of Agriculture, and his able staff, particularly Marion Montague.

My research was greatly helped by the cooperation of Warren J. Haas, Director of Libraries at Columbia University, Cornelius McKissic of the National Agricultural Library in Beltsville, Md., Professor Morton Rothstein of the University of Wisconsin at Madison, and Professor Tom G. Hall of California State College at Hayward. My thanks also go to Thordis J. Boyle and Irene Weaver of Washington, D. C., for their unstinting assistance in locating and supplying statistical data.

Patricia Gozzi is due warm praise for the skill and industry with which she cheerfully deciphered and typed page after page of my tortured drafts.

Finally, I wish to thank my wife, Maria Luisa Fornari; she not only patiently put up with the customary travails of a business-man's wife, but was also an intellectual companion providing stimulus when due and encouragement when needed. To her, therefore, this book is dedicated.

H. F.

List of Illustrations

A closeup of floor traders in action.
Cargo unloading at Port Bunge, Minnesota.
Maturing soybean plants in Missouri.
Tugboat pushing grain-laden barges at East St. Louis, Illinois.
Loading grain in barges at East St. Louis, Illinois, 1959.
Grain inspectors sampling grain near East St. Louis, Illinois.
Wheat from Duluth elevator being loaded into a freighter, 1945.
The laker A. T. Kinney, July 1960, loading corn in Chicago.
Barges hauling corn through New York State Barge Canal to Albany, June 1941.
Milled rice being brought from Lake Charles Port Storage to the docks.
The *Linfield Victory*.
Aerial view of a section of National Defense Reserve Fleet anchored in the Hudson River.
Grain transported from the Midwest being loaded at Baltimore, Maryland.
The Manhattan.
Wheat being loaded into the *Manhattan*.

Following page 158

Bunge's export elevator at Destrehan, Louisiana.
Rear view of Bunge's Destrehan elevator.
Grain testing, using a divider.
Removing weed seeds, using hand sieves.
Grading wheat.
Testing moisture content of a grain sample.
The *Quebec*.
Europoort Silo, N.V., completed in 1972.
Grain being loaded at Europoort Silo, N.V.
Closeup of the pneumatic discharge towers at Europoort Silo, N.V.
Wheat is unloaded in the port of Goa, India, January, 1966.
U.S. wheat, newly arrived in Bombay, India, May 1959.
U.S. Wheat being unloaded at a port in Pakistan.
Cultivator near the village of Varanasi, Uttar Pradesh, India.
Modern 10,000 ton grain storage facility completed in 1959 at Hapur, Uttar Pradesh.
Warehouse at a grain elevator in Calcutta built in 1966.
U.S. grain being loaded for transport to Ethiopia.
American food and feed being unloaded at a port in Jordan in 1963.

I

Corn from the Colonies

The month was October, the year 1625. It was barely five years since the Mayflower voyagers, after making their landfall at what is now Provincetown, had finally come ashore on Plymouth Rock. And, according to the first American historian, Governor William Bradford, it had only been in April, 1621, that they had begun "to plant ther corne, in which servise Squanto stood them in great stead, showing them both ye manner how to set it, and after how to dress and tend it." [1] For three years, in fact, the Plymouth Colony had been on the verge of starvation and had had to resort to purchasing grain from the Indians and to stringent rationing of these supplies. [2] Now, however, they had a bumper crop. A shipwright sent to Plymouth from England in 1624 had built "two very good and strong shalops . . . and a great and strong lighter," [3] and the colonists loaded one of these boats with corn and sent it north to the Kennebec River, where it was exchanged for seven hundred pounds of beaver and other furs. [4] The outward movement of American grain had begun.

It was, of course, only a token shipment, and at least two more decades would have to elapse before a true export trade could be developed. Meanwhile, the colonists in the sparse settlements along the Atlantic seaboard endeavored to expand cultivation and production of grains, meeting with very uneven results. They may well have wondered about the basis for the enthusiasm of Arthur Barlowe, who, reconnoitering the North Carolina coast for Walter Raleigh in 1584, had noted in his journal that "the earth bringeth forth all things in aboundance, as in the first creation, without toile or labour." [5]

The reason for the initial failures of the pioneering English settlers, despite the fertility of the soil and the generally favorable climate, must be found in their understandable insistence on trying to raise those crops and use those farming methods with

1

which they had been traditionally acquainted in England. In any event, the colonists soon adopted the Indian technique of girdling and burning trees to clear new fields, and resorted to planting Indian corn, or maize, as the one crop which had the best chance of success and also gave a better yield than European grains. The latter, of course, were also tried at one time or another, and eventually became important crops. Wheat, by 1640, was well established in New England, where it was made acceptable in payment of taxes, just as Indian corn had been made legal tender for debts in 1631.[6] Connecticut was especially successful in wheat production, although the success was short-lived as a result of the black stem rust which began to affect wheat fields in eastern Massachusetts around 1660 and soon spread throughout New England. The middle colonies (New York, the Jerseys, and later Pennsylvania) also grew wheat in large volume, which accounts for their eventually coming to be called the "bread colonies." Rye was grown along the Delaware, where the Swedes had established a settlement in 1638, and barley and oats also became well and widely established. All of these grains were referred to cumulatively as "corn" according to the Old English usage, while what we today call simply corn was then characterized as "Indian."

As immigration increased and settlements multiplied, there were still occasional instances of shortages, relieved by shipments from one colony to another. In 1631, for example, John Mason's plantation on the Piscataqua River received seven hundred bushels of corn from Virginia,[7] and three years later as much as ten thousand bushels came from the same origin to the Massachusetts Bay Colony.[8]

By the middle of the seventeenth century, however, New England was at the peak of its brief period of activity as exporter of its own grain surplus. The Connecticut valley was raising abundant wheat crops. Connecticut grain was moving to Boston in volume, giving rise, in fact, to protests by the farmers of the Plymouth and Massachusetts Bay Colonies, who, as farmers before and after them, often complained of abnormally low prices. In 1644, as a result, the general court in Hartford granted to certain merchants the exclusive right to export grain, hoping that they would ship it to foreign markets and thus sustain domestic prices. This they proceeded to do with such success that in 1650 a chronicler of the Massachusetts Bay Colony could write that:

. . . those who were formerly forced to fetch most of the bread they eat, and beer they drink, a hundred leagues by Sea, are through the blessings of the Lord so encreased, that they have not only fed their Elder Sisters, Virginia, Barbados, and many of the Summer Islands . . . but also the Grandmother of us all, even the firtil Isle of Great Britain, beside Portugal hath had many a monthful of bread and fish from us, in exchange of their Madeara liquor, and also Spain.[9]

There was undoubtedly some exaggeration in Johnson's boasts, as, except in periods of crop failure, most European markets were generally still too far for American grain. The islands of the West Indies, however, be they English, Dutch, or French, provided a natural outlet for the surplus corn and wheat of New England and the middle colonies. It would have been uneconomical for the sugar planters of the Caribbean to devote to the production of foodstuffs land and labor which could be much more profitably employed in raising their staple crop, and they eagerly bought their requirements from New England as well as from the middle colonies. As early as 1643 a traveler in New Netherland wrote from Peter Stuyvesant's town that ". . . three large ships of three hundred tons each had come to load wheat; two found cargoes, the third could not be loaded, because the savages had burnt a part of the grain. These ships had come from the West Indies. . . ." [10] And in 1678 Governor Andros reported annual exports from New York of over sixty thousand bushels of wheat, primarily to Caribbean destinations.[11]

By the last quarter of the seventeenth century, New Jersey and Pennsylvania were developing as strong competitors in the West Indian grain trade, while in New England wheat cultivation virtually ended and her colonies increasingly turned to bringing in grain, both for domestic consumption and for reexport after conversion into meal or flour. "This," wrote a contemporary observer referring to east New Jersey, "with the Province of *New York* being the *Granary* or *Store House* of the *West Indies,* without which *Barbadoes* and the *Leeward Islands* could not subsist; yea, *New England* is forced to come there every year for Corn." [12]

Lest it appear that the expanding colonial export trade in grain as well as in all other commodities was allowed to proceed without regulation from the mother country, a brief outline of such regulation seems desirable. The economic controls which were introduced into the English colonies were rooted in English experience and stemmed from a body of doctrine called "mercantilism," which had as its objective the creation of a prosperous national state or self-sufficient empire. Such prosperity and power were to be gained by maintaining an ample stock of precious metals, protecting home industries against foreign competition, and making it possible for home industries to compete successfully in foreign markets through the availability of the necessary raw materials from the colonies and the maintenance of low production costs by providing subsistence labor.

Mercantilism, with its emphasis on the primacy of money as wealth, had gained ascendancy in the sixteenth century, when the discoveries in the new world had led to a great development of the European currencies. In the seventeenth century, the Netherlands took the lead in foreign commerce, since the Italians had been deprived of their earlier preponderance by the opening of the new maritime routes, and Germany and Spain were otherwise occupied by long-drawn wars and internal squabbles. In France, Colbert based his entire expansionistic policy on the mercantilist system, while in England, where, under the early Stuarts, colonial economic development had been left by Parliament to the Crown, Cromwell caused Parliament to enact legislation which destroyed the Dutch carrying trade and founded the British empire of the sea.

The first of the many Acts of Trade and Navigation, as they were called, was passed on October 3, 1650, and it simply prohibited foreign vessels from carrying goods to or from the colonies without a special license. A year later, on October 9, 1651, a more comprehensive act stipulated, among other restrictions, that no goods from Asia, Africa, or America could be imported into England, Ireland, or the colonies except in British-owned ships manned by predominantly British crews, and that no European goods could be carried to those destinations except in English ships or ships of the country of origin.

At the outset, this legislation, which was to be followed by a plethora of supplementary restrictions throughout the balance of the colonial period and was to contribute in no small measure to the eventual clash between England and her American colonies, could hardly be enforced, because of the lack of British shipping to replace the Dutch. In 1652 and again in 1656 the governors of Barbados and Antigua complained of supply shortages and petitioned for repeal of the Act of 1650. In 1655 the Virginia Assembly declared that it would maintain freedom of trade and protect its merchants. In addition, at various times between 1655 and 1660, Massachusetts, Rhode Island, and Connecticut publicly proclaimed that they would continue to trade with the Dutch.

Nevertheless, no sooner had Charles II been restored to the throne than he approved, on October 1, 1660, a new navigation act providing that nothing could be exported from or imported into any English colony except in English-built or English-owned vessels, of which the captain and three-fourths of the crew were to be English. This act also initiated the listing of "enumerated" articles of colonial origin which could only be shipped to England or her colonies, further stipulating that vessels leaving colonial ports must post bond to guarantee that they would carry the "enumerated" goods to England and nowhere else. Other navigation acts followed in 1662, 1663, 1673, and 1699, generally reaffirming and expanding the controls and restrictions on colonial trade and establishing procedures for their enforcement.

With specific regard to the export of grain from the colonies, the effect of the navigation acts was subject to interplay with other English legislation, namely, the Corn Laws. While grain could be freely imported into Great Britain from any origin until 1463, that year a statute was passed which set forth specified price levels for various grains and prohibited importation when domestic markets fell below such levels, stating, as the basis for the restrictions, that ". . . . the laborers and occupiers of husbandry in England were daily put to a grievous loss by the importation of corn from other lands. . . ."[13] This act had been repealed in 1624, as the intervening rise in domestic price levels from the original schedules had long since made it outdated. In 1663, however, in an obvious effort to encourage English agriculture, the Restoration Parliament reestablished minimum price levels for grains and decreed that heavy duties were to be paid on imported grains whenever prices at home were lower than the minimum.

While this act and others on the same subject which followed it in later years met with varying success because of the difficulty of establishing reliable price determinations, one definite result of the Corn Laws and the navigation acts was to prevent the importation of American cereals into England, thus compelling the colonists to export their surplus to other overseas markets.

These markets were primarily in the West Indies and in southern Europe, that is, Portugal, Spain, and their island possessions in mid-Atlantic. As early as 1648, John Winthrop, explaining a shortage of wheat in Massachusetts, wrote: "Our scarcity came by occasion of our transporting much to the West Indies and the Portugal and Spanish Islands." [14]

Well before the end of the seventeenth century, New England was no longer a surplus producer of grain. Nevertheless, through its predominance in shipbuilding and shipping, New England long continued to retain the lion's share in the export trade, of which shipments of grain acquired from other colonies constituted a sizable portion.

Consideration of New England's trade patterns is generally epitomized in the most famous "triangle," which began with the shipment of rum to Africa where it was exchanged for slaves, who were then carried across the infamous "middle passage" to the West Indies and there sold for cash, sugar, and molasses. The latter were taken back to New England to be manufactured into more rum and thus permit the first leg of a new triangle to begin. Another triangle was "the shipment of provisions . . . to the West Indies. The goods were exchanged there for sugar and molasses, which were then carried to England, where they were sold to buy manufactures for the return voyage, or frequently the ship was sold in England. Lastly, a ship might carry fish, wheat, and lumber to southern Europe to be exchanged for wine, salt, and fruits, sail to England to exchange these for manufactures, and then return to the Colonies." [15] The most recent scholarship, however, indicates that shuttle routes far overshadowed triangular ones, both in numbers of vessels engaged and in tonnage transported. These specialized trade routes, in order of importance, primarily connected the "bread colonies" with Great Britain, New England with the West Indies, and the upper south with southern Europe.[16]

By 1700, New York and Philadelphia, whose grain exports had been predominantly handled by Yankee merchants, were endeavoring to establish overseas connections and engage in direct trading. That year William Bolton, an English factor on Madeira Island, remarked on the arrival of more vessels from Pennsylvania and New York than from New England, and wrote: "This place hath been abundantly supply'd with all sorts of Provisions, soe that . . . Wheate cannot be shipped from England—because of the coming of soe many vessels from the Westerne Colonies." [17]

By the end of the seventeenth century the West Indian market was glutted with flour and bread from colonial Pennsylvania.[18] In 1703, however, the Treaty of Methuen between England and Portugal opened the latter country to surplus American grain, and Pennsylvania merchants were quick to take advantage of the opportunity. Only eight years later, Isaac Norris of Philadelphia could write: "I am apt to think the country has, within ten or twelve years, increased to near ten times its then produce of corn, wheat especially. The market of Lisbon has been of great advantage to us." [19]

Wheat exports from the middle colonies to southern Europe were not always remunerative, as is most clearly expressed in an official report forwarded to London from New York in 1734. The report, which strikingly reflects some of the woes besetting grain shippers of any time or country, stated:

> Wheat is the staple of this Province, and tho' that commodity seem literally to interfere with the product of Great Britain, It do's not so in fact, for its generally manufactur'd into flower and bread, and sent to supply the sugar Collonys, And whenever a Markett in Spain Portugal or other parts of Europe has encouraged the sending it thither in Grain, the Adventurers have often suffered by the undertaking, for at this remote distance, the intelligence of a demand reaches us so late, that the marketts are supplyed before our Vessells come there, and even if it were otherwise our Merchants lye under vast and certain disadvantages besides for freight of Wheat from hence in time of warr was at least two shillings and six pence, and in time of peace is eighteen pence Sterling per bushell and by the length of the passage it often grows musty at least cannot come so fresh to Market as from Great Britain; whence freights (as its said) are not above one quarter part of what they are at here.[20]

One might wonder why colonial merchants persisted, but it seems logical that even when Polish, English, or Sicilian competition for the grain market kept prices low, American shipments were still made in order to secure cash and bills of exchange to pay English creditors. When debts were pressing, a cargo of grain sent to Spain or Portugal could answer such demands.[21] Indeed, as was noted by a Pennsylvania correspondent of the English Board of Trade in 1716, a main reason why that colony had "shipt large quantities of corn to Portugal and other parts of Europe [was] to put themselves in a capacity of purchasing in England cloathing and other necessaries which they want." [22]

It was in this period that a most interesting scheme to stimulate grain exports was formulated, more than two centuries before the Commodity Credit Corporation and the New Deal's farm support programs appeared on the American scene. The plan was contained in a 1725 book by Francis Rawle, a prominent Philadelphia trader, entitled *Ways and Means for the Inhabitants of Delaware to Become Rich*. By "Delaware" the author meant the territory on both sides of the river, now comprising the states of Pennsylvania and Delaware, but then one proprietary colony. Rawle claimed that "the true cause of our Poverty and sunk Condition is the low Price of our Country Produce," and referring to "that Specie which is the Chief Staple of our Trade, *Wheat* . . . what we raise in vast Quantities and what we are most to depend on," he urged on "the Legislative Authority of the Provinces on Delaware, that a Bounty per Bushel be paid for all Wheat which shall be exported to any Parts of the Continent of Europe; as to France, Spain, Portugal and . . . Italy." Such an export subsidy could be financed by means of "a Land-Tax or a Duty on Rum," according to Rawle, who went on to characterize his scheme as "the only means to advance the Price of Grain which of late has been so low, that the Farmer has been reduc'd to the Brink of Ruin . . .", and to point out that "if the Planter or Farmer sinks, the Merchant or Trader cannot swim." [23]

Even though nothing came of Rawle's scheme, the volume of grain exported from the American colonies increased consistently during the eighteenth century, and the destinations expanded to include all Spanish Mediterranean ports and the west coast of Italy. In 1731, Pennsylvania alone shipped over fifty-five thousand bushels of grain to Ireland and southern Europe.[24]

The wars between England and France which had begun with King William's War in 1689 and progressed, with a peaceful interlude from 1713 to 1739, to the final settlement of the Anglo-French rivalry in the French and Indian War and the Peace of Paris in 1763, of course had their influence on the grain export trade as well as on all other aspects of colonial life and administration. Supplies were at times requisitioned to provision military units, and vessels on the high seas were subject to seizure by French privateers or warships. Prices rose steadily. Wheat, which in 1756 had sold at Philadelphia for 3.36 shillings per bushel, cost 5.42 shillings in 1763. Corn prices during the same years were 2.11 and 3.69 shillings per bushel respectively. Then, beginning in 1764, a series of poor harvests forced England to become a grain-importing rather than a grain-exporting nation. European countries formerly supplied with English grain immediately turned to the English colonies in America to fill the deficit. On February 19, 1766, the British Parliament modified the Corn Laws to permit the duty-free importation of American grains. English grain traders sought American wheat and corn for their home markets and also to satisfy their contracts with foreign buyers. Poor crops in various parts of Europe in 1766 gave further impetus to the demand for American grain.[25]

"In Consequence of the Scarcity and Dearness of Provisions in Europe," wrote a New Yorker at the end of 1766, ". . . upwards of Twenty sail of European ships arrived last week in different Ports of America, in order to purchase Wheat. This must of Consequence raise the Price of Wheat and other Provisions upon us, already too high for the Poor of this City. . . . If those ships get their Loads of Wheat, it will benefit farmers that have it to sell, but it must impoverish the Citizens, in advancing the Price of Provisions."[26]

The continuing expansion of grain exports was indeed generally acknowledged to be the primary cause of soaring prices and food shortages in the towns at this time, and colonial authorities endeavored to regulate markets and control speculation by a number of measures, none of which achieved more than temporary results.

Baltimore emerged at this time as a port from which substantial quantities of wheat were shipped to England, while sizable exports of corn were made from Virginia. Philadelphia, however, remained the largest grain exporting center, followed in that order by New York and Boston. From April, 1765, to April, 1766, Philadelphia's exports comprised 367,522 bushels of wheat and 168,426 barrels of flour, each barrel being the equivalent of 4½ bushels of wheat. Flour, in fact, gradually became relatively more

9

important, so that in 1772, for example, the Quaker city shipped to the West Indies only 92,012 bushels of wheat but 284,872 barrels of flour.[27]

We have so far dealt exclusively with the principal grains exported, namely, wheat and corn, it being understood, of course, that they were primarily shipped in processed form, the wheat as flour or biscuit and the corn as meal. Two other items, however, must be mentioned, as they eventually achieved considerable importance. Rice, first introduced in South Carolina in 1694 from seed imported from Madagascar, quickly became an export commodity, with Portugal and the West Indies as principal outlets. As an indication of the fast expansion of rice cultivation, it is worth noting that in 1696 an act of the South Carolina Assembly already included rice as one of the commodities which would be accepted for certain public payments.

As has been wittily noted, "ordinarily the [British] government did not subject a colonial activity to regulation by law until it had proved itself to be profitable," [28] and indeed in 1705 rice was added to the list of "enumerated" commodities which could only be shipped to England to be eventually reexported from there after payment of duty. There was undoubtedly a certain amount of smuggling, but it was not until Parliament in 1730 permitted direct shipments of this grain to destinations south of Cape Finisterre that exports resumed in large volume, with one-quarter to one-half of the annual crop being sent to southern Europe, primarily Portugal and Spain, but with substantial quantities also going to Holland, Germany, Denmark and Sweden. Exports from Charleston rose from eighteen-hundred barrels of six hundred pounds each in 1700 to forty-five thousand in 1734, ninety thousand in 1755, and 110,000 in 1773. Savannah shipped two thousand barrels of rice in 1755, and twenty-four thousand in 1772.

Another principal grain export in the eighteenth century was flaxseed or linseed. Before 1700 all the hemp and flax used in Great Britain were imported from Holland and the Baltic countries. Beginning in that year, however, and at various other times during the balance of the colonial period, subsidies were granted for American-grown flax, and production expanded considerably, first in New England and later in New York. Writing from Manhattan in 1748 an English traveler stated:

They send ships to Ireland every year, laden with all kinds of West India goods but especially with linseed, which is reaped in this province. I have been assured, that in some years no less than ten ships have been sent to Ireland, laden with nothing but linseed; because it is said the flax in Ireland does not afford good seed. But probably the true reason is this: the people of Ireland, in order to have the better flax, make use of the plant before the seed is ripe, and therefore are obliged to send for foreign seed and hence it becomes one of the chief articles in trade.

At this time a bushel of linseed is sold for eight shillings of New York currency or exactly a piece of eight.[29]

In 1770, more than 300,000 bushels of flaxseed were shipped to England and Ireland from the colonies.

Meanwhile, however, British policy towards the colonies was changing. The growing export trade of New England and the middle colonies was cause for alarm to the English mercantilists. It built up in the colonies a merchant class that threatened to compete successfully with English traders and shipowners, and thus nullify those features of the navigation acts which aimed to center in England most of the trade of English America.[30]

Soon after the end of the French threat to the English colonies, their inhabitants became increasingly loath to pay taxes for the maintenance of a defense establishment no longer needed. Great Britain, in turn, resorted to increasingly restrictive policies, expressed in such galling legislation as, among others, the Quartering Act, providing for the billeting of British troops in the colonists' homes, the well-known Stamp Act and Townshend Acts, imposing various taxes, and, in 1775, the New England Restraining Act, forbidding first the New England colonies, and then several others, to trade with any nation except Great Britain and excluding New Englanders from the North Atlantic fisheries.

The colonists' reaction was naturally rebellious. In essence, the American colonists, "having lived so long under the rule of mercantilism, had become imbued with mercantilist ideas. If the British imperium would not allow them to grow and expand . . . the colonists would have to take to themselves the right and the power to guide their economic development . . . to create a new authority that would foster American shipping and commerce. . . ."[31]

Fanned by political as well as economic grievances, the spirit of

11

independence gained momentum. The inevitable clash between the colonies and the mother country eventually occurred, and the fledgling republic set out to shape its own destiny.

Notes To Chapter I

1. William Bradford, *History of Plymouth Plantation*, ed., W. T. Davis (New York: C. Scribner's Sons, 1908), p. 100.
2. *Ibid.*, pp. 138, 150, 157.
3. *Ibid.*, p. 120.
4. *Ibid.*, p. 210.
5. D. B. Quinn, editor, *The Roanoke Voyages 1584-1590.* Quoted in Edmund S. Morgan, "The Labor Problem at Jamestown, 1607-18", *The American Historical Review*, Vol. 76, No. 3 (June 1971), p. 598.
6. W. B. Weeden, *Social and Economic History of New England 1620-1789* (Boston and New York: Houghton, Mifflin and Company, 1890), p. 101.
7. John Ward Dean, editor, *Capt. John Mason* (Boston: The Prince Society, 1887), p. 62.
8. Weeden, *Social and Economic History*, p. 128.
9. J. Franklin Jameson, editor, *Johnson's Wonder Working Providence, 1628-1651* (New York: C. Scribner's Sons, 1910), p. 247.
10. Quoted in Percy Wells Bidwell and John I. Falconer, *History of Agriculture in the Northern United States 1620-1860* (New York: Peter Smith, 1941), p. 45.
11. Everett E. Edwards, "American Agriculture—The First 300 Years," *Yearbook of Agriculture—1940* (76th Congress, 3rd Session—House Document No. 695), pp. 187-188.
12. Quoted in Bidwell and Falconer, *History of Agriculture*, p. 45.
13. Normal Scott Brien Gras, *The Evolution of the English Corn Market From the Twelfth to the Eighteenth Century* (New York: Russell & Russell, 1967), p. 148.
14. John Winthrop, *Winthrop's Journal*, "History of New England," 1630-1649, ed., James K. Hosmer (New York: C. Scribner's Sons, 1908), II, p. 341.
15. Gary M. Walton, "New Evidence on Colonial Commerce," *Journal of Economic History*, XXVIII, No. 3 (Sept. 1968), pp. 363-364.
16. *Ibid.*, pp. 365-366.
17. Quoted in James G. Lydon, "Fish and Flour for Gold: Southern Europe and the Colonial American Balance of Payments," *Business History Review*, XXXIX, No. 2 (Summer, 1965), p. 177.
18. Anne Bezanson, Robert D. Gray, and Miriam Hussey, *Prices in Colonial Pennsylvania* (Philadelphia: University of Pennsylvania Press, 1935), p. 9.
19. *Ibid.*
20. Quoted in Bidwell and Falconer, *History of Agriculture*, p. 134.
21. Lydon, *Fish and Flour*, p. 179.
22. *Ibid.*, p. 178.
23. William Renwick Riddell, "Suggested Governmental Assistance to Farmers Two Centuries Ago, in Pennsylvania," *Pennsylvania Magazine of History and Biography*, LIII (1929), pp. 137-138.
24. Mary A. Hanna, *The Trade of the Delaware District Before the Revolution* (Northampton, Mass.: Dept. of History of Smith College, 1917), p. 264.
25. William S. Sachs, "Agricultural Conditions in the Northern Colonies Before the Revolution," *The Journal of Economic History*, XIII, No. 3 (Summer, 1953), pp. 284-285.
26. *Pennsylvania Gazette*, November 13, 1760. Quoted in Sachs, "Agricultural Conditions," p. 287.
27. Sachs, "Agricultural Conditions," p. 286, *n.* 37.
28. Curtis P. Nettels, "British Mercantilism and the Economic Development of the Thirteen Colonies," *The Journal of Economic History*, XII, No. 2 (Spring, 1952), p. 108.
29. Quoted in Bidwell and Falconer, *History of Agriculture*, p. 134.
30. Nettels, "British Mercantilism," p. 111.
31. *Ibid.*, p. 114.

II

Antebellum Seesaw

Like most wars, the American Revolutionary War had unforeseen results. Although at least in part triggered by the American colonists' opposition to British attempts to tax them and limit their commerce, the war not only gained independence for them but also caused a rise in taxation and a contraction of foreign trade.[1]

With specific regard to the production and export of agricultural commodities, there is no doubt that the war brought about widespread disorganization and imposed the need of a major market reorientation. The situation which prevailed in this field during the American Revolution is very graphically described in a letter sent in 1787 to his superiors by the British consul in Philadelphia. "During the troubles," he wrote,

> . . . a number of useful labourers were taken from the pursuits of agriculture and employed as soldiers; the diminution of useful labour occasioned a diminution of the crops and the farmer sustained a heavy loss thereby . . . a very considerable discouragement to agriculture existed during the war, the intercourse with Europe and the West Indies was so frequently obstructed by the cruizers that the farmer found no certain vent for his produce and fearful that the little he raised might perish on his hands he looked scarcely further than to the nurture of his family and became careless of cultivating more than their wants required . . . farm houses fell into decay, so that upon the accession of peace those means which were formerly exerted for the purpose of tillage and improvement were appropriated to the discharge of old debts. . . .[2]

For the foreign grain trade, independence meant that the former colonies were excluded from the mercantilist system governed by the British Navigation Acts, and that, therefore, certain markets

15

would henceforth be closed to American exports. At the same time, the end of hostilities and the signing of the Treaty of Paris in 1783 resulted in the cession by England to the United States of vast new territories which greatly expanded the potential agricultural productivity of the new nation. The treaty gave the United States all territory east of the Mississippi except Florida, and the northern part of these newly acquired lands, bounded by the Great Lakes, the Ohio River, and on the west by the Mississippi River, comprised about 240,000 square miles, or an area almost three-fourths that of the original thirteen colonies. In 1787 they were organized by the Confederation Congress into the Northwest Territory and eventually became the states of Ohio, Indiana, Michigan, Illinois, and Wisconsin. It was these new virgin regions, together with some of those acquired through the Louisiana Purchase two decades later, which, by the middle of the nineteenth century, became the veritable granary of America, providing food for a quickly expanding population as well as strong backing for the nation's foreign trade. Before that stage was reached, however, a long and difficult process of development was required, involving gradual settlement, technical innovations, and a true revolution in transportation facilities and marketing techniques. It is the latter factors that are most relevant to the purposes of this study, but before considering them it is appropriate to review briefly the highlights of the export grain trade in the intervening period.

While, before the war, the American colonies had virtually monopolized the supply of foodstuffs to the British West Indies, the end of hostilities brought about the exclusion of United States vessels from the carrying trade to those destinations. In 1788, in fact, an act of Parliament had imposed most stringent restrictions, so that the West Indies were forced to depend primarily upon British or Canadian grain. As a result, total value of exports from the United States to the British West Indies fell from an annual average of $2.2 million in 1771-1773 to $1.4 million in 1785-1787 and to $1.2 million in 1793. It is interesting to note, however, that the trade in grain did not suffer in the same proportion, and in fact, exports of biscuit and flour actually increased slightly.[3]

When war broke out between England and France, American grain began to find its way into the West Indies, violating in every way the British commercial system,[4] and while, according to the official records, there were no shipments to the British West Indies between 1788 and 1793, a substantial amount of smuggling took place, either directly or through transshipment at the French or Dutch possessions in the Caribbean. Bona fide commerce with these possessions also took place in growing volume, with American ships developing a new triangular trade which took corn to the French West Indies, coffee and sugar from there to Europe, and manufactured goods back to the United States. In any event, after 1793 the British planters succeeded in obtaining a relaxation of the Act of 1788, and American ships were once again admitted to the islands.[5]

Great Britain itself, which was intermittently dependent on grain imports for her own needs as well as eager to facilitate export of her manufactured goods, was from the beginning open to American grain, provided, as stipulated in Jay's Treaty of 1794, the grain was carried in British ships or in American-built and American-owned vessels of which the master and three-fourths of the crew were American citizens.

By 1793 Liverpool was becoming the main center of England's trade with America, and was with London one of the two primary grain ports in the British Isles. Of course, it was also most important for cotton and tobacco, which were, after all, much greater in value and tonnage than grain.

It has been said that in the history of the British import trade in grain, no country looms more important than the United States. [6] This statement, which was made almost fifty years ago, no longer holds true, as a result of the intervening vast expansion of Canadian agriculture. During the entire period of the Napoleonic Wars, however, Canada was but a small and undependable source of supply, and she was, in fact, a frequent importer of grain from the United States. It was indeed to America that Great Britain turned for substantial percentages of her food supply in the Napoleonic era, especially after 1799 when a catastrophic crop failure caused widespread famine and bread riots throughout Great Britain. Altogether, 620,872 bushels of wheat were imported from the United States into England in 1800, and over 2 million bushels the following year.[7] Writing to his government early in 1801, the British consul at Philadelphia noted that "Almost every large ship upon her arrival in the Delaware is taken up for the purpose of conveying flour to England," and remarked on the "monstrous price" commanded by American flour.[8] Prices had naturally been rising, so that by June, 1801, superfine flour was quoted at Virginia ports at almost $11.00 per barrel.[9] The year 1802 brought temporary peace between France and England through the Treaty of Amiens, as well as a bumper crop in England, resulting in a 50 percent reduction in English imports and an almost equal drop in prices. Wheat, which had averaged in Britain 14 shillings a bushel in 1801, was down to 8½ by November, 1802.[10]

In May, 1803, the new outbreak of hostilities with France caused a renewed interest in American grain. American wheat and flour poured into British ports to the extent of 873,000 bushels or about one-fourth of all the wheat and flour imported by England in 1803. Another plentiful harvest in Britain that autumn brought this trade to a standstill, so that for all of 1804 only thirty-five thousand bushels of wheat came to England from America, and only slightly over one hundred thousand bushels the following year.

Napoleon's victories at Jena and Auerstadt in 1806 prevented the shipment of Prussian grain to England, and American grain was once more called in to fill the gap. As a result of the seesawing of supply and demand, prices also fluctuated widely, but imports of American wheat in 1806 were larger than from any other origin except Ireland.

The prosecution of the war in Europe, and the political maneuvering which enmeshed both belligerents and neutrals, now saw the beginning of a period of increased friction between Great Britain and the United States which ultimately resulted in the War of 1812 and which, in the meantime, seriously affected trade between the two nations. Since the resumption of the Napoleonic Wars in 1803, both England and France had clamped restrictions on neutral commerce aimed at depriving each other of food and war supplies.

Since the British navy by far surpassed the French in numbers and power, it was British interference with American ships which constituted the more serious offense against neutral rights. Thus by 1806 Anglo-American relations had already been strained for some time by the restrictions which Great Britain sought to place on United States freedom of commerce and navigation. The Jay Treaty had expired early in 1806, and negotiations for a new treaty had begun when, in November, Napoleon issued the Berlin Decree which was designed to isolate England by cutting the lifeline of her seaborne trade. The British government, in turn, asked

18

James Monroe and William Pinkney, whom Jefferson had sent to London to negotiate a new trade pact, to request that the United States force France to respect the right of neutral shipping or join England in opposing Napoleon. Without waiting for an answer, however, the English government published a series of Orders in Council, which made every American vessel subject to search and seizure, and which resulted in the notorious *Chesapeake* affair. American public opinion was naturally incensed, and President Jefferson countered by proclaiming an embargo which Congress approved in December, 1807. Fortunately for grain traders on both sides of the Atlantic, shipments for that year had been completed, with 1,998,000 bushels of wheat going from the United States into Great Britain out of her total imports of 3,239,-000. In 1808, however, with the embargo in full force, the figure was down to 103,000 bushels of wheat.

The embargo, which virtually prohibited all foreign commerce, was easily circumvented, and a brisk smuggling trade sprang up in grain as well as in other commodities. Nevertheless, volume of shipments suffered considerably. While, for instance, in 1807 the United States had exported to all destinations 1,018,721 bushels of corn and 136,360 barrels of corn meal, in 1808 the corresponding figures were a mere 249,533 bushels and 30,818 barrels.[11]

Opposition to the embargo was therefore widespread and vocal, not only from the Federalists in Congress but also from the mercantile interests in New England and New York. As a result, in March, 1809, the embargo was repealed and replaced with the Non-Intercourse Act which reopened trade with all foreign countries except Great Britain and France. Soon thereafter, relying on the assurance of the British ambassador that the Orders in Council would be repealed, President Madison authorized by proclamation resumption of trade with Great Britain, and a flood of American grain sailed toward the British Isles and was unloaded there. At the end of May the British Foreign Secretary disavowed his ambassador's action, and accordingly in August Madison revived the Non-Intercourse Act against Great Britain. Despite the act's being in force during most of 1809 and half of 1810, however, England received from America almost 1,400,000 bushels of wheat in 1809, and substantial quantities the following year. Of course, this trade was illegal and was accomplished either by transshipment through the Iberian Peninsula or by various subterfuges. A report by the American consul at Bristol in 1810 is clearly indicative of one technique used by many American traders and shipowners in evading the Non-Intercourse Act. "American subjects," the consul wrote,

> will continue to arrive at our different ports with the product of the United States after (in general) first touching at Ferol, Madeira etc., getting Portuguese Papers, changing their names and also that of their masters, and then proceeding in the double capacity of both nations with registers and other documents of each . . . You will observe one of these in the British Mercury enclosed, registered for Lisbon under the name of 'Neuston Senora dor Nanto L. J. N. . . . Mastre.' This ship loaded with tobacco, flour, etc., at Bermuda Hundred in Virginia, called at Madeira, underwent the usual transformation, came here where her cargo was landed and sold, is in fact the American ship Bristol Trader, Captain Gilbert belonging to New York, between which Port and this port she has been employed for several years past.[12]

In May, 1810, the obviously unenforceable Non-Intercourse Act was replaced by a bill which reopened trade with both England and France, further stipulating that if either country should revoke its restrictions against American shipping, the president would prohibit trade with the other. When Napoleon ambiguously indicated that certain of his restrictive decrees would be canceled, Madison naively accepted the French declarations at face value, and in November proclaimed that unless England repealed her Orders in Council by March, 1811, Non-Intercourse would once more be enacted. The ensuing debates and exchanges of charges and countercharges on both sides of the Atlantic, as well as the intensified harassment of American vessels by British warships and the resulting incidents, are beyond the scope of this study, as is the actual course of the war between the United States and Great Britain which occupied the second half of 1812 and all of the following two years. What must be noted is that although the war brought to a complete standstill the direct export of American grain to Great Britain, the slack was taken up by vastly increased shipments to the Iberian Peninsula. Exports of American wheat and flour to Spain and Portugal, where the British and French were struggling for supremacy, had already shown sharp advances in 1811 and 1812, but the peak was reached in 1813 when America shipped to the Iberian Peninsula almost one million barrels of flour as well as three hundred thousand bushels of wheat, for a total value of over $11 million.[13]

It is also interesting to note that throughout the War of 1812, New England and New York contractors regularly supplied flour as well as other provisions to the British armies in Canada as well as to English warships off the East Coast.

While, from the beginning of the Napoleonic Wars to the War of 1812, Great Britain was supplied with American grain and flour primarily from ports on the eastern seaboard, it was New Orleans which during the same period carried on a substantial share of exports to the West Indies and to Central and South America. The Mississippi River, which between 1784 and 1787 had been closed by Spain to all foreign ships, and had only been reopened to Americans in 1788 subject to a 15 percent export duty, was made freely navigable to American vessels by the Treaty of San Lorenzo in 1795. The same agreement authorized the establishment at New Orleans of a free zone deposit for American goods. In 1798 such a deposit was opened there, a fact which, when coupled with Spain's opening of Havana and other colonial ports to neutral shipping, explains the quick growth of New Orleans as an export point for American grain at the turn of the century. Until the beginning and development of the transportation revolution, New Orleans constituted the only export outlet for grain and provisions from the Northwest Territory. Flour was the principal item exported, with ninety thousand barrels in "some 470 flatboats and keels . . . reported passing or embarking from Cincinnati" in 1801, and similar quantities the following two years.[14] Despite its coming under American sovereignty through the Louisiana Purchase in 1803, during the subsequent decade, hampered by the British blockade in the Caribbean as well as by the eventual restrictions of embargo, Non-Intercourse, and war, the New Orleans grain export trade declined, so that between 1804 and 1814 only about 225,000 barrels of flour were shipped abroad from New Orleans. It is significant, however, that of this quantity almost one-half went to the West Indies, and one-fifth to Central America and west Florida.[15]

The end of the war and the signing of a trade treaty with Great Britain in July, 1815, brought about a revival of the export grain trade, and with it a land boom which, fostered in part by an exceptional demand from Europe after poor harvests there in 1817, lasted until the panic of 1819.

In a country which was still primarily agricultural, however, foreign commerce in grain still represented a rather small fraction of total exports, due primarily to the difficulties of transportation to seaboard. In 1817 a report to the New York Legislature indicated that the expense of transporting goods from Buffalo to New York was $100 per ton, so that the cost of transportation equaled nearly three times the market value of wheat in New York, and six times the value of oats.[16]

As to the pioneers who, since the opening of the Territory, had moved into the Northwest—270,000 of them by the 1810 census—the only way to move their surplus production to market was through the Ohio-Mississippi river system, a route available only to those sections of Ohio, Indiana, and Illinois watered by tributaries to the Ohio or Mississippi. Even the farmers who used those waterways were faced at New Orleans with an unpredictable grain market. Actually, bulk cereals formed a negligible part of exports, since grain was mainly shipped in concentrated form— flour, pork, lard, whiskey—which could better stand the cost of freight and were easier to handle.[17]

Consequently, at this time the vast majority of grain growers in the United States were still virtually restricted to raising only what they needed for their families or could sell in the immediate neighborhood to obtain what minimum cash they required. The heavy cost of transportation worked against the farmers, not only in shrinking the return for their products, but also in raising the cost of their supplies. As late as 1820, a farmer who brought his wheat and flour to Pittsburgh had to give up a bushel and a half of the former and a whole barrel of the latter to obtain one pound of coffee or tea respectively. In Ohio the purchase of a pair of boots called for the value of twenty bushels of wheat, while in Kentucky wheat sold for twenty cents and corn for ten cents a bushel. Flour from central Pennsylvania, when brought to Baltimore, netted the wheat grower only $1.25 a barrel. The same barrel of flour, when exported to Cuba, paid into the Spanish treasury a duty of $4.75. Similar customs barriers existed in most of the potential foreign markets. Another obstacle to cultivation expansion was the wave of agitation for legislative devices which tried to maintain the fictitious values created by the land boom that had raged from 1815 to 1819. "Evidently the United States could not look forward to any considerable exportation of the food products of the interior until the expenses of transportation should be greatly decreased, the tariff restrictions on their importation into foreign countries in some degree relaxed, and the overcapitalization of its farm lands much reduced. These hindrances to economic prosperity confronted over half the population of the country. . . ."[18]

The second of these conditions did not begin to be fulfilled until much later, and the third never permanently was, so ingrained in the American character was the fever to "buy land cheap and sell it dear." But the transportation revolution was now about to begin, and with it the chain reaction of ever-growing westward expansion which had as a major result the eventual emergence of the United States as the world's major producer and exporter of grain.

Road building was the first manifestation of the need and desire of the coastal areas to tap their hinterlands as sources of agricultural products and markets for finished goods, and of the demand of inland growers for better outlets for their crops. Between 1790 and 1820 literally hundreds of private companies were organized to build toll roads, and they did establish a sizable network of such turnpikes. Since private capital was obviously inadequate to fill the need for new roads, the federal government was pressured into intervention, and in 1808 Treasury Secretary Albert Gallatin submitted to Congress an extensive report advocating the construction of roads and canals with public funds, which resulted in eventual construction of the Cumberland Road, connecting Cumberland, Maryland, with Vandalia, Illinois, 834 miles away.

Despite the improved roads, overland traffic was still generally too slow and expensive, especially for the transportation of farm products. On the Mississippi and Ohio, even though steamboats had first appeared in 1812 and had rapidly gained in popularity and numbers, downstream traffic was still carried out primarily by thousands of flatboats and keelboats, and as settlement and agricultural production of the West increased, the river traffic could no longer fill the needs of the expanding new regions. Adequate interstate transportation facilities were essential to the further growth of both eastern industrialization and western agriculture, and the new era was opened by the building of the Erie Canal.

Begun in 1817, "Clinton's ditch" joined Buffalo to Albany in 1825 and paid for itself in nine years. The cost of shipping a ton of freight from Buffalo to New York was cut from $100.00 to $15.00, and the transit time from twenty days to eight. The value of farm products in western New York doubled, and there was a corresponding increase in the northwest. New York City soon became the foremost American seaport, its population increasing about 60 percent between 1820 and 1830. The tie thus knotted between the northeast and the northwest had an enormous impact on the development of the United States.[19]

Another route linking west to east was opened a few years later, in 1833, by the Welland Canal, which bypassed Niagara Falls from the Canadian side, making it possible for lake vessels to go past the Falls and then sail to Oswego, a port on Lake Ontario, from which point the Oswego Canal provided a connection to the Erie Canal and ultimately to New York.[20]

Other states quickly followed suit, and over the next two decades extensive canal systems were built in Pennsylvania, Indiana, and Illinois, through the organization of stock companies by promoters who, with dazzling promises of high revenues from toll charges, set off a veritable craze of canal building. For the eastern North Central states, the availability of the eastern market caused increased production, accelerated westward migration, and expanded land cultivation. The northwest was no longer dependent on a glutted New Orleans market, and western wheat began to feed not only industrial America but England as well.[21]

Although the first B&O train was built in 1828 and its first eleven miles of rail laid by 1830, railroads did not substantially expand beyond the Alleghenies until the middle of the century. It should be recorded at this time, however, that a notable change was taking place in ocean transportation.

Between 1600 and 1800, while the carrying trade of more valuable goods had been virtually monopolized by fleets of large and well-armed Dutch and British East Indiamen, grain and provisions were transported as full cargoes by much smaller ships such as barks, *pinasses*, brigantines, and schooners, whose capacity varied from as little as 150 to not more than 300 tons. By the beginning of the nineteenth century, however, larger ships were being built, and these increasingly offered to carry parcels of grain, acting in effect as common carriers. Furthermore, starting around 1820 both British and American shipowners established packet lines linking American and European ports on regular schedules, and it became possible for a New York merchant to know that his shipment of flour would be loaded on board on a preannounced day and delivered in Liverpool three to four weeks later. Finally, beginning in the 1820s, the successful application of steam as a means of propulsion and the increasing use of iron in building ships' hulls opened a new era in merchant shipping.

The years 1815-1818 marked a period of great activity in grain exports, not to be matched again until the early 1830s, and then sharply declining again until the end of that decade. A primary cause of the reduced significance of American grain exports was the fact that, with the westward shift of cultivation and the resulting trend towards urbanism and industrialization in the East, the domestic market was expanding more rapidly and steadily than foreign demand. Another basic hindrance to a sustained level of grain exports was the fact that, although the United States did enjoy a dominant position as supplier to certain markets such as Cuba, the West Indies, and parts of South America, the largest potential customer, Europe, was only interested in American grain when crop failures or wars drastically reduced her own resources. As has been concisely outlined, ". . . Europe was an accidental market to the American grain grower. It was not more than that on account of the competitive handicaps of the United States." [22] These handicaps were indeed many and serious. Compared with tenant labor in England or serf labor in Russia or Prussia, farm labor in the United States was far more expensive. Compared with the cheap river transportation enjoyed by grain growers of northern Europe, inland transportation in America was also much too costly, whether it be down the Mississippi or through the Great Lakes and the Erie Canal. Even the length of the ocean voyage to England from New Orleans or New York put American shippers at a disadvantage against the much shorter trip from Danzig or Hamburg.

A graphic representation of United States grain exports in the seven decades before the Civil War, therefore, shows a wildly fluctuating pattern, the peaks of which are easily identified as relating to European crises, such as the Napoleonic Wars, the Irish Potato Famine, or the Crimean War.

From 1835 to 1837, in fact, because of early frosts and generally poor harvests in the United States, there were numerous instances of wheat and oats being imported into New York from

England and Prussia.[23] At the same time, with the growing demand in Europe for American cotton, returning vessels slashed their freight rates rather than sail in ballast, and part of their cargo consisted of European grain, which was landed and sold in the New Orleans market in competition with American grain.[24]

These were, of course, exceptions of minor significance, well overshadowed by the progress being made in this period both in the removal of barriers to international trade and the technical improvements in cultivation and handling of grain.

Trade agreements were made in 1828 with Sweden, Norway, Brazil, Guadeloupe and Martinique, and the following year with Prussia; with Great Britain and Canada in 1830, in 1831 with Austria-Hungary, in 1832 with Spain, Mexico, and Russia, and in 1836 with Portugal, Madeira, the Azores, Venezuela and Tuscany.[25] The agreement of 1830 with Great Britain opened the British West Indies to American grain, primarily in the form of corn and corn meal as food for the sugar plantation workers.

Between 1815 and 1860 corn and corn meal represented only from 10 to 15 percent of the total value of grain exports, with the exception of the peak period of 1845-1849 when the corn average percentage reached 29. Also, until 1850, wheat accounted for less than 10 percent of the value of grain exports, while wheat flour was by far the main export item.[26] In fact, from 1800 to 1845 the percentage of wheat exported in the form of flour was never less than 90 percent. From 1846 onwards, owing to a number of factors such as improvements in European milling techniques, tariff differentials, and lower railroad export rates favoring wheat over flour, the proportion began to shift, but by 1860 it was still 67 percent of the total.[27]

As to technical improvements, this period saw the development of the steel plow, essential to cultivation of the matted prairie soil, and, in 1831, the construction of Cyrus McCormick's first reaper. Even more important for the purpose of our study, the first grain elevator ever successfully built anywhere was installed at Buffalo in 1843.

Flour and meal were exported in barrels, which could be easily manipulated, and their concentrated value more easily justified the expenditure of the necessary labor. Wheat, however, was generally shipped in bags, an awkward method which hardly lent itself to the shipment of the vast amounts of grain which were beginning to move in commercial channels by the 1840s. With the grain trade expanding into the heart of the American continent, it became necessary to transfer the commodity at several points on the way to the seaboard. This hindrance was particularly serious on the Great Lakes-Erie Canal route, where relatively higher labor costs increased the difficulties.[28]

While the wheat traffic down the Mississippi continued to be carried out in bags until after the Civil War (which undoubtedly contributed to New York supplanting New Orleans as the principal grain port after 1846), beginning in the mid-1830s grain shipped eastward from the northwest was generally shipped in bulk in the canal or lake boats, by emptying into the vessel's hold the bags in which it came from the farm. Once the lakers from the West arrived at the transfer points for the Erie Canal, Buffalo and Oswego, the grain had to be unloaded, weighed, and either stored or transferred directly to canal boats for the trip to the Hudson River and New York. It was here that the major bottleneck occurred, for, in the words of the man who two years later was to own the first successful elevator, as late as 1841:

> . . . the universal method of transfer was to raise the grain from the hold of the vessel, in barrels, by tackle and block, to weigh it with hopper and scales swung over the hatchway of the canal boat, or carry it into the warehouse in bags or baskets, on men's shoulders . . . Only ten or fifteen bushels were commonly weighed at a draft; and the most that could be accomplished in a day, with a full set of hands, was to transfer some eighteen hundred or two thousand bushels, and this only when the weather was fair. Everything was at a standstill in bad weather; and, on an average, one-fourth of the time was lost by rain or high winds. The harbor was often crowded with vessels, waiting for a change of weather.[29]

The solution was eventually found, as is often the case, by the adaptation and refinement of an existing device. In 1780, not content with having invented a machine for carding wool and cotton, Oliver Evans had joined his brothers in operating a flour mill in Delaware, and, among other labor-saving appliances, he had designed a way of raising wheat to the top of the mill's storeroom. This consisted of an endless belt, on vertical pulleys, with small iron buckets attached at regular intervals. Once in motion, with mules or horses supplying the power, the buckets would scoop the wheat from a hopper into which bags had been emptied. At the top of their journey, the buckets would dump it into chutes from where it would flow to the bins. Several attempts were made to utilize Evans' device in the unloading of grain from vessels moored alongside a warehouse, at Buffalo in 1837, at Toledo in 1838, and at Chicago in 1841 and 1842. The first truly successful elevator, however, was the one built at Buffalo in 1843 by a young Scotsman, Robert Dunbar, who would eventually become a world-famous authority on grain handling. Operated by a steam engine, Dunbar's contrivance utilized the principle of Evans' bucket elevator, and extended out from the warehouse so that it could be lowered into the hold of a vessel moored alongside. Its initial capacity was a thousand bushels an hour, which was soon doubled by means of adjusting the buckets more closely on the chain.

This new mechanical system of handling grain quickly spread throughout the various Great Lakes ports, and

> the association of the grain elevator and the grain warehouse became so common that the warehouses began to be called simply "grain elevators." The elevators did more than unload grain. They were built with huge bins for storage and often were equipped with devices for the cleaning and screening of grain. Grain was stored pending shipment or while the owner was waiting for an improvement in the market. The elevators were built so that the storage bins were located high enough to facilitate the unloading of grain by action of the force of gravity.[30]

Most of the grain which flowed from the hinterlands was still primarily intended to feed the growing urban population of the industrialized eastern seaboard, but undoubtedly the growth of the elevator system was also of vital importance to the export trade, and made it possible for American grain to be more available to fill foreign demand when it experienced one of its occasional spurts.

Such an event occurred in 1846-47. Great Britain, which in 1828 had enacted a Corn Law based on the old principles of the navigation system, setting a sliding scale of duties on breadstuffs in order to protect domestic grain growers, was confronted by a crisis of unprecedented gravity when heavy rains ruined her grain crops in the fall of 1845. Coming on top of the potato blight, which in the same year had destroyed Ireland's staple food crop, and followed by an even worse crop failure in the Emerald Isle the following year, England's plight threatened to reach famine proportions. As a result, Sir Robert Peel's government, which for many years had been resisting the agitation for repeal of the protective duties fanned by the industrialists who sought cheaper bread for their laborers, had no choice but to bow to the combined pressure of the Anti-Corn Law League and of the hungry populace, and in June, 1846, threw British ports open to foreign grain. Harvests had also been reduced by floods in northern Europe, and France, Belgium and Holland in turn lifted their customs barriers to permit grain imports.[31]

The net result for the American foreign trade in grain was that wheat exports jumped from less than half a million bushels in 1845 to almost 4.5 million in 1847, while exports of flour in the same years went from 1.2 to 4.4 million barrels. The greatest increment was shown by corn, total exports of which rose from less than 1 million bushels in 1845 to more than 16 million in 1847.[32] "And yet," stated an official U. S. Government report,

> this large quantity sent to foreign countries did not exhaust our surplus products by millions of bushels. On a tour through several of the States bordering on the great western lakes, during the last summer, the undersigned found the depots of grain, the remains of the crops of 1846, filled to overflowing, and all the avenues of transportation choked up with the immense quantities which were pouring through them to the Atlantic coast to seek markets abroad. It will not exceed the truth to say that the surplus of grain in this country, and particularly of maize, is sufficient to meet any demand which all the corn purchasing countries of Europe combined can make upon us under any probable circumstances . . . The only difficulties to be encountered, would be the inadequate means of transportation from the interior to the coast, and ships to carry our surplus product across the Atlantic.[33]

It is interesting to note that since American wheat could enter Canada free of duty from 1831 to 1843, and at a very minimal rate from 1843 until the Corn Laws were repealed in 1846, flour milled in Canada from American grain enjoyed a notable advantage over its competitors from other origins. Canadian exports to Britain had in fact comprised in large part American grain, since Canada still had a negligible exportable surplus. In this respect, repeal of the Corn Laws in England represented a loss to American exports, since Canadian shipments were now forced to compete with all others on equal terms. Shipments from Canada to Great Britain, which had averaged slightly over 2 million bushels a year from October, 1843, to June, 1846, were cut in half during the period 1848-1853.[34]

A beneficial effect of both the Corn Law repeal and expanded imports of American grain into Great Britain, on the other hand, was the opportunity afforded the British government to allay English resentment of the Oregon Treaty, by which in 1846 the territory below the forty-ninth parallel was definitely ceded to the United States. American war-hawks, rallying to the slogan "54°: 40' or fight," had for years agitated for greater territorial gains, while many Englishmen had rejected the notion of making any concession at all. The issue had caused considerable tension on both sides of the Atlantic, and its settlement was facilitated by the greater need to face and solve the British food emergency.

Meanwhile the range of destinations for American grain, especially flour, was widening. In 1839 substantial shipments were made to China and Argentina, and to Mexico, the Philippines, Australia, Turkey, Scandinavia, Africa, Tuscany, Sicily, and Sardinia in the following decade. Brazil was for many years a major market for American flour. The leading importers of American wheat and flour were England and her Western Hemisphere colonies, especially Canada, while most American corn went to England, Ireland, and the West Indies, the latter also being a main market for corn meal. Most of the American exports of rye went to Australia, Canada, England, Belgium and the British West Indies.

The westward population movement was also progressing at an increasing pace. Settlement had spread in the 1830s across Indiana, Michigan, Illinois, and Wisconsin, and between 1840 and 1850 the grain-producing states of Iowa and Wisconsin had been admitted into the Union, and the Territory of Minnesota had been organized. All of these began producing wheat for sale, marketing it eastward through the Lakes and southward down the Mississippi.

Until 1850, the internal commerce of the country was conducted almost entirely through water lines—natural and artificial, and over ordinary highways. By 1860, however, eight trunk line railroads served as outlets for the products of the interior.[35]

It was undoubtedly the advent of the railroads, the Vermont Central in 1850, the New York & Erie in 1851, and the New York Central in 1853, which resulted in New York's becoming the major export center in the country, while the Pennsylvania and the Baltimore & Ohio gave increment to export expansion and trade rivalry between Philadelphia and Baltimore. Equally important in enlarging the supply base at its source, other railroads were built throughout the Eastern North-Central states in a seemingly endless pattern. "Expanding population and production were inextricably bound up with the construction of thousands of miles of railroads, reaching out from ambitious Lake Michigan ports into their immediate hinterlands, beyond to the Mississippi River, and eventually to the trans-Mississippi West."[36]

The rapid growth of the railroads, accompanied as it was by waves of land speculation, was instrumental in opening up new areas to cultivation and in increasing production of grain which could now more economically and expeditiously be moved to market. The new method of transportation also spurred the growth of secondary receiving centers such as Toledo, Milwaukee, and, above all, Chicago. Furthermore, the advent of the railroad affected all aspects of the grain trade. Shipping grain to Chicago was much quicker and safer, and since it now arrived there in large volume and cars had to be unloaded quickly for a fast turnaround, it became necessary for the railroads to build large grain elevators with automatic equipment. "It further required that grain be carried by grade from the original point of departure and stored by grade at the secondary market, rather than being handled, as it was in the 1840s, in separate units as numerous as there were owners of grain."[37]

By the mid-1850s Chicago had become the unrivaled center of the interior grain trade, and, thanks to its improved connections with the exporting outlets on the eastern seaboard, it was able to take full advantage of the sudden demand created in Europe at that time by poor harvests and especially by the outbreak of the Crimean War in March, 1854. British wheat imports averaged in this period about 20 million bushels a year, and, as a firm of British merchant bankers wrote to their American correspondent a few weeks after war had been declared, "they could not see where [England could] look for a future supply (with the Baltic & Black Seas closed) except to the United States and Canada."[38]

Napoleon III was also anxious to accumulate reserve stocks of grain in France to tide the country over the war emergency. As a result, total American exports once more spurted to new highs. From 1854 to 1857 more than 30 million bushels of wheat, 12 million barrels of flour, and 33 million bushels of corn left American ports for foreign destinations.[39] The British need for American grain played a part in England's ultimately conciliatory attitude in the controversies then involving the two countries over the Mosquito Islands and other Central American territories as well as over fishery rights and trade reciprocity.[40]

The end of the Crimean War caused American grain exports to contract once more, and with reduced exports came sharply lower market prices, which were in part a cause of the panic of 1857. These price declines were wholly disproportionate to the relative importance of export volume to volume of total harvest. It was indeed true, as a trade writer had editorialized in 1846, that "the selling price of the whole of the grain produced in this country, is regulated almost entirely by what we can obtain for the small portion that we succeed in finding a foreign market for—and which never amounts to one-twentieth of what we raise!"[41]

For instance, when news of the large English demand in 1846-47 reached Cincinnati, flour prices quickly moved from $3.00 a barrel to more than $5.00. During the Crimean War, wheat prices in Chicago were pushed to over $1.40 a bushel. New York flour prices, which had been relatively stable at around $4.50 a barrel through 1852 and part of 1853, jumped to $7.75 in January, 1854, and by September had risen to $9.87, only to fall back to less than $5.00 a barrel by 1858. As has been tersely stated, "The very irregularity of the market was sufficient to throw a port into a state of feverish and often impetuous activity whenever any chance bit of information was received hinting at English short-ages. . . ."[42]

The fluctuations were of course not fully reflected in the aver-age prices, which nevertheless showed appreciable variations from year to year, as shown by a tabulation for the seventy-year period under review. The percentage of total exports represented by grain was also widely irregular.

While wheat, flour, and corn represented by far the largest

percentage of American grain exports during this period, some mention should be made of other grains which were also contributing to the total export volume. Rye, oats, and barley, as grain, represented a negligible fraction of shipments throughout this period. Rye flour, on the other hand, though of minor importance in relation to the main breadstuffs, was exported in appreciable if widely fluctuating quantities. The lowest level in the seven decades under review was reached in 1809, with exports of 1,306 barrels, and the highest in 1818, when over 107,000 barrels were exported. Flaxseed exports averaged about 200,000 bushels a year until 1830, declining to an annual average of 100,-000 bushels between 1830 and 1846, and almost disappearing thereafter. Rice, on the contrary, exhibited a remarkable stability in its export volume; such exports averaged from 80,000 to 120,-000 tierces of six hundred pounds each, every year during the entire period.[43]

As we have seen, the overall importance of grain exports, even though fluctuating in volume, was continually growing in its influence on market prices as well as expansion of production. It is not surprising, therefore, that in the mid-1850s an Ohio editor would boast that ". . . not all the laws under heaven can prevent this great West from becoming to the Old World what Sicily was to Rome—the grand granary." [44]

It would be more than two decades before this prophecy would be realized, however. Meanwhile, the cannon fire in Charleston Bay, which touched off the Civil War, opened a new chapter in the American saga.

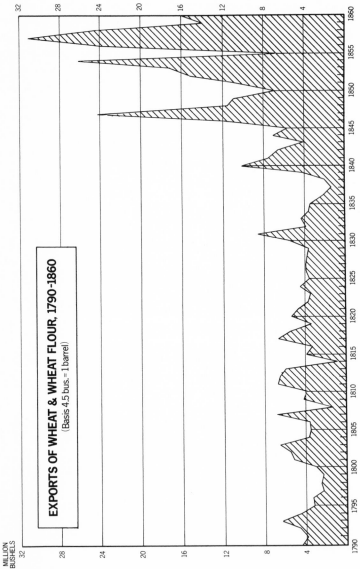

MILLION BUSHELS

EXPORTS OF WHEAT & WHEAT FLOUR, 1790-1860

(Basis 4.5 bus. = 1 barrel)

Fig. 1. (Sources: Charles H. Evans, "Exports, Domestic and Foreign from the American Colonies to Great Britain, from 1697 to 1789, Inclusive. Exports, Domestic and Foreign from the United States to All Countries, from 1789 to 1883, Inclusive." **House Miscellaneous Documents,** 48 Cong. 1 Sess. No. 49, Part 2 (1884), Serial 7236, pp. 20-23, 113-116.)

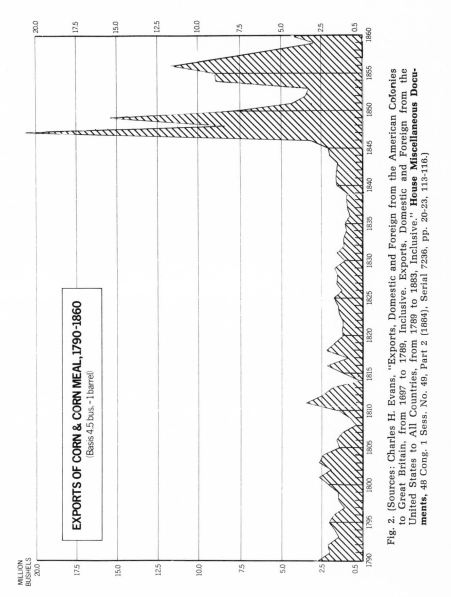

MILLION BUSHELS

EXPORTS OF CORN & CORN MEAL, 1790-1860

(Basis 4.5 bus. – 1 barrel)

Fig. 2. (Sources: Charles H. Evans, "Exports, Domestic and Foreign from the American Colonies to Great Britain, from 1697 to 1789, Inclusive. Exports, Domestic and Foreign from the United States to All Countries, from 1789 to 1883, Inclusive." **House Miscellaneous Documents**, 48 Cong. 1 Sess. No. 49, Part 2 (1884), Serial 7236, pp. 20-23, 113-116.)

TABLE 1—TOTAL EXPORTS OF

(000 omitted)

Year	Bulk Wheat (bus.)	Wheat Flour (brls.)	Grain Equiv. of Flour (bus.)	Total (bus.)
1790	1,124	725	3,262.5	4,386.5
1791	1,018	620	2,790.0	3,808.0
1792	854	824	3,708.0	4.562.0
1793	1,451	1,075	4,837.5	6,288.5
1794	696	846	3,807.0	4,503.0
1795	141	687	3,091.5	3,232.5
1796	31	725	3,262.5	3,293.5
1797	16	516	2,322.0	2,338.0
1798	15	568	2,556.0	2,571.0
1799	10	519	2,335.5	2,345.5
1800	27	653	2,938.5	2,965.5
1801	240	1,102	4,959.0	5,199.0
1802	280	1,156	5,202.0	5,482.0
1803	686	1,312	5,904.0	6,590.0
1804	127	810	3,645.0	3,772.0
1805	18	778	3,501.0	3,519.0
1806	87	783	3,523.5	3,610.5
1807	1,173	1,250	5,625.0	6,798.0
1808	87	264	1,188.0	1,275.0
1809	394	846	3,807.0	4,201.0
1810	326	798	3,591.0	3,917.0
1811	217	1,445	6,502.5	6,719.5
1812	54	1,443	6,493.5	6,547.5
1813	289	1,261	5,674.5	5,963.5
1814	...	193	868.5	868.5
1815	18	863	3,883.5	3,901.5
1816	52	729	3,280.5	3,332.5
1817	96	1,479	6,655.5	6,751.5
1818	197	1,158	5,211.0	5,408.0
1819	82	751	3,379.5	3,461.5
1820	22	1,177	5,296.5	5,318.5
1821	26	1,056	4,752.0	4,778.0
1822	4	828	3,726.0	3,730.0
1823	4	757	3,406.5	3,410.5
1824	20	997	4,486.5	4,506.5
1825	18	814	3,663.0	3,681.0
1826	45	858	3,861.0	3,906.0
1827	22	868	3,906.0	3,928.0

WHEAT AND FLOUR, 1790-1860

Year	Bulk Wheat (bus.)	Wheat Flour (brls.)	Grain Equiv. of Flour (bus.)	Total (bus.)
1828	7	861	3,874.5	3,881.5
1829	6	837	3,766.5	3,772.5
1830	45	1,227	5,521.5	5,566.5
1831	523	1,801	8,104.5	8,627.5
1832	93	865	3,892.5	3,985.5
1833	32	956	4,302.0	4,334.0
1834	40	835	3,757.5	3,797.5
1835	48	779	3,505.5	3,553.5
1836	2	505	2,272.5	2,274.5
1837	17	319	1,435.5	1,452.5
1838	6	448	2,016.0	2,022.0
1839	96	923	4,153.5	4,249.5
1840	1,721	1,898	8,541.0	10,262.0
1841	869	1,516	6,822.0	7,691.0
1842	818	1,284	5,778.0	6,596.0
1843	312	841	3,784.5	4,096.5
1844	559	1,439	6,475.5	7,034.5
1845	390	1,195	5,377.5	5,767.5
1846	1,614	2,289	10,300.5	11,914.5
1847	4,400	4,382	19,719.0	24,119.0
1848	2,035	2,119	9,535.5	11,570.5
1849	1,528	2,108	9,486.0	11,014.0
1850	609	1,385	6,232.5	6,841.5
1851	1,027	2,202	9,909.0	10,936.0
1852	2,695	2,799	12,595.5	15,290.5
1853	3,890	2,921	13,144.5	17,034.5
1854	8,037	4,022	18,099.0	26,136.0
1855	799	1,205	5,422.5	6,221.5
1856	8,155	3,511	15,799.5	23,954.5
1857	14,570	3,712	16,704.0	31,274.0
1858	8,926	3,512	15,804.0	24,730.0
1859	3,002	2,432	10,944.0	13,946.0
1860	4,115	2,612	11,754.0	15,869.0

(Sources: Charles H. Evans, "Exports, Domestic and Foreign from the American Colonies to Great Britain, from 1697 to 1789, Inclusive. Exports, Domestic and Foreign from the United States to All Countries, from 1789 to 1883, Inclusive." *House Miscellaneous Documents,* 48 Cong. 1 Sess. No. 49, Part 2 (1884), Serial 7236, pp. 20-23, 113-116.)

TABLE 2—TOTAL EXPORTS OF CORN

(000 omitted)

Year	Bulk Corn (bus.)	Corn Meal (brls.)	Grain Equiv. of Meal (bus.)	Total (bus.)
1790	2,102	100	450.0	2,552.0
1791	1,713	70	315.0	2,028.0
1792	1,965	53	238.5	2,203.5
1793	1,234	38	171.0	1,405.0
1794	1,506	49	220.5	1,726.5
1795	1,935	103	103.0	2,038.0
1796	1,173	120	540.0	1,713.0
1797	805	57	255.0	1,060.0
1798	1,218	47	212.0	1,430.0
1799	1,200	51	231.0	1,431.0
1800	1,694	73	338.0	2,032.0
1801	1,768	204	919.0	2,687.0
1802	1,633	59	267.0	1,900.0
1803	2,080	134	603.0	2,683.0
1804	1,945	111	499.5	2,444.5
1805	862	116	522.0	1,384.0
1806	1,064	108	486.0	1,550.0
1807	612	136	612.0	1,224.0
1808	250	31	139.5	389.5
1809	522	57	256.5	778.5
1810	1,054	87	391.5	1,445.5
1811	2,791	147	661.5	3,452.5
1812	2,040	91	409.5	2,449.5
1813	1,487	59	265.5	1,752.5
1814	61	26	117.0	178.0
1815	831	72	324.0	1,155.0
1816	1,077	...	1,077.0	2,154.0
1817	387	107	481.5	868.5
1818	1,675	120	540.0	2,215.0
1819	1,087	135	607.5	1,694.5
1820	534	146	657.0	1,191.0
1821	607	132	594.0	1,201.0
1822	509	148	666.0	1,175.0
1823	749	142	639.0	1,388.0
1824	779	153	688.5	1,467.5
1825	870	187	841.5	1,711.5
1826	505	159	715.5	1,220.5
1827	978	131	589.5	1,567.5

AND CORN MEAL, 1790-1860

Year	Corn (bus.) Bulk	Corn Meal (brls.)	Grain Equiv. of Meal (bus.)	Total (bus.)
1828	705	175	787.5	1,492.5
1829	898	174	783.0	1,681.0
1830	444	145	652.5	1,096.5
1831	571	208	936.0	1,507.0
1832	451	147	661.5	1,112.5
1833	487	147	661.5	1,148.5
1834	303	150	675.0	978.0
1835	756	167	751.5	1,057.5
1836	125	141	634.5	759.5
1837	151	159	715.5	866.5
1838	172	172	774.0	946.0
1839	162	166	747.0	909.0
1840	574	206	927.0	1,501.0
1841	535	232	1,044.0	1,579.0
1842	600	209	940.5	1,540.5
1843	672	174	783.0	1,455.0
1844	825	248	1,116.0	1,941.0
1845	840	269	1,210.5	2,050.5
1846	1,826	299	1,345.5	3,171.5
1847	16,326	948	4,266.0	20,592.0
1848	5,818	582	2,619.0	8,437.0
1849	13,257	405	1,822.5	15,079.5
1850	6,595	259	1,165.5	7,760.5
1851	3,427	204	918.0	4,345.0
1852	2,627	181	814.5	3,441.5
1853	2,275	212	954.0	3,229.0
1854	7,769	257	1,156.5	8,925.5
1855	7,808	267	12,015.0	9,009.5
1856	10,292	294	1,323.0	11,615.0
1857	7,505	268	1,206.0	8,711.0
1858	4,766	238	1,071.0	5,837.0
1859	1,720	259	1,165.5	2,885.5
1860	3,314	234	1,053.0	4,367.0

(Sources: Charles H. Evans, "Exports, Domestic and Foreign from the American Colonies to Great Britain, from 1697 to 1789, Inclusive. Exports, Domestic and Foreign from the United States to All Countries, from 1789 to 1883, Inclusive." *House Miscellaneous Documents,* 48 Cong. 1 Sess. No. 49, Part 2 (1884), Serial 7236, pp. 20-23, 113-116.)

TABLE 3—AVERAGE EXPORT PRICES OF WHEAT,

Year	Wheat bus.) ($ per	Wheat Flour ($ per brl.)	Corn (¢ per bus.)	Corn Meal ($ per brl.)
1790	1.24	6.50	NA	3.00
1791	1.00	5.50	NA	2.00
1792	NA	NA	NA	NA
1793	NA	NA	NA	NA
1794	NA	NA	NA	NA
1795	NA	NA	NA	NA
1796	NA	NA	NA	NA
1797	NA	NA	NA	NA
1798	NA	NA	NA	NA
1799	NA	NA	NA	NA
1800	NA	NA	NA	NA
1801	NA	NA	NA	NA
1802	NA	NA	NA	NA
1803	NA	NA	75.6	NA
1804	NA	NA	102.3	NA
1805	NA	NA	104.3	NA
1806	1.33	8.00	83.0	NA
1807	1.25	7.00	80.6	NA
1808	1.25	6.50	76.8	NA
1809	1.25	6.00	70.3	NA
1810	1.50	7.50	79.0	NA
1811	1.75	9.50	83.9	NA
1812	1.94	10.00	79.2	NA
1813	1.75	11.00	105.1	NA
1814	NA	9.50	95.5	NA
1815	1.25	8.00	98.8	NA
1816	1.75	10.00	NA	NA
1817	2.25	12.00	150.0	7.00
1818	2.00	10.00	100.0	5.50
1819	1.26	8.00	75.0	4.50
1820	.75	4.50	62.0	3.50
1821	.81	4.07	43.0	2.62
1822	.70	6.16	74.3	3.52
1823	1.32	6.56	60.9	3.37
1824	1.02	5.77	45.1	2.52
1825	1.03	5.17	49.4	2.39
1826	.86	4.80	76.2	3.92
1827	.67	5.09	60.1	3.31

40

FLOUR, CORN AND CORN MEAL, 1790-1860

Year	Wheat ($ per bus.)	Wheat Flour ($ per brl.)	Corn (¢ per bus.)	Corn Meal ($ per brl.)
1828	.76	4.98	48.6	2.75
1829	1.59	6.91	53.3	2.85
1830	1.02	4.95	50.6	2.56
1831	1.30	5.50	69.4	2.87
1832	1.06	5.64	61.8	3.27
1833	.92	5.87	69.3	3.64
1834	1.07	5.41	67.1	3.29
1835	1.08	5.64	77.8	3.77
1836	1.00	7.06	83.1	4.41
1837	1.57	9.37	97.8	4.79
1838	1.29	8.04	82.3	4.20
1839	1.50	7.50	86.9	3.97
1840	.95	5.35	58.9	3.42
1841	.95	5.12	58.4	2.94
1842	1.12	5.75	57.5	2.95
1843	.85	4.47	41.9	2.61
1844	.90	4.70	49.0	2.59
1845	.86	4.52	49.0	2.38
1846	1.04	5.09	64.1	3.16
1847	1.37	5.96	88.2	4.53
1848	1.31	6.22	66.0	3.10
1849	1.14	5.35	60.1	2.89
1850	1.06	5.12	59.0	2.93
1851	1.00	4.78	51.4	3.06
1852	.95	4.24	58.6	3.17
1853	1.12	5.06	60.4	3.35
1854	1.55	6.89	78.2	3.90
1855	1.66	9.04	89.2	4.63
1856	1.85	8.34	74.1	4.00
1857	1.53	6.97	69.1	3.58
1858	1.02	5.50	68.4	3.69
1859	.95	5.93	76.9	3.84
1860	.98	5.92	72.4	3.90

Sources: Charles H. Evans, "Exports, Domestic and Foreign from the American Colonies to Great Britain, from 1697 to 1789, Inclusive. Exports, Domestic and Foreign from the United States to All Countries, from 1789 to 1883, Inclusive." *House Miscellaneous Documents,* 48 Cong. 1 Sess. No. 49, Part 2 (1884), Serial 7236, (pp. 20-23, 113-116.)

Table 4—Dollar Value of Grain Exports Compared to Exports of Other Products, 1837-1860

(000 omitted)

Year	Grain	Cotton	Tobacco	Manufactures	Total	Grain Percent of Total
1837	8,821	63,240	14,659	7,836	94,556	9.33
1838	6,765	61,557	7,392	8,483	84,197	8.03
1839	11,005	61,239	9,833	10,928	93,005	11.83
1840	15,588	63,870	9,884	11,848	101,190	15.40
1841	12,377	54,330	12,577	13,523	92,807	13.34
1842	11,904	47,593	9,541	10,941	79,979	14.88
1843	6,956	49,120	10,920	7,462	74,458	9.34
1844	11,239	54,064	8,397	10,618	84,318	13.33
1845	9,811	51,740	7,470	12,480	81,501	12.04
1846	19,330	42,767	8,478	12,439	83,014	23.29
1847	57,070	53,416	7,242	11,613	129,341	44.12
1848	25,186	61,998	7,551	14,475	109,210	23.06
1849	25,642	66,397	5,804	12,207	110,050	23.30
1850	15,372	71,985	9,951	17,243	114,551	13,42
1851	16,877	112,315	9,219	32,207	170,618	9.89
1852	19,883	87,966	10,031	56,301	174,181	11.42
1853	23,793	109,456	11,319	46,148	190,716	12.48
1854	51,191	93,596	10,016	26,180	180,983	28.28
1855	23,651	88,144	14,712	28,027	154,534	15.30
1856	59,391	128,382	12,129	30,129	230,031	25.82
1857	58,333	131,576	20,261	30,140	240,310	24.27
1858	35,925	131,387	17,010	30,243	214,565	16.74
1859	24,047	161,435	21,074	33,758	240,314	10.01
1860	27,590	191,207	15,807	39,574	274,178	10.06

(Source: Wunderlich, "The Foreign Grain Trade," p. 42)

Notes To Chapter II

1. George Rogers Taylor, "American Economic Growth Before 1840: An Exploratory Essay," *The Journal of Economic History,* XXIV, No. 4 (December, 1964), p. 437.
2. Phineas Bond to Lord Carmarthen, May 17, 1787. Quoted in Gordon C. Bjork, "Weaning the American Economy: Independence, Market Changes, and Economic Development," *Journal of Economic History,* XXIV, No. 4 (December, 1964), p. 546.
3. Bjork, "Weaning the American Economy," p. 552.
4. W. Freeman Galpin, *The Grain Supply of England During the Napoleonic Period* (New York: The Macmillan Company, 1925), p. 4.
5. S. G. Checkland, "American Versus West Indian Traders in Liverpool, 1793-1815," *The Journal of Economic History,* XVIII, No. 2 (June, 1958), p. 143, n.3.
6. Galpin, *The Grain Supply,* p. 135.
7. *Ibid.,* p. 136. The quantities given above and in the following pages, when only related to wheat without specific mention of flour, are actually representative cumulatively of bulk wheat as well as flour, the latter in fact constituting the largest part of the total. A ratio of 4.5 bu. wheat = 1 bl. flour is used. Also, the quantities originally expressed in "quarters" have been converted at the ratio of 1 quarter = 8 bushels.
8. Phineas Bond to Grenville, March 1, 11, 1801. Quoted in Galpin, *The Grain Supply,* pp. 136-137.
9. *Alexandria* (Va.) *Advertiser,* June 27, 1801.
10. Galpin, *The Grain Supply,* p. 33.
11. Timothy Pitkin, *A Statistical View of the Commerce of the United States of America* (New Haven: Durrie & Peck, 1835), p. 102.
12. Consular Despatches, Bristol, May 10, 1810. Quoted in Galpin, *The Grain Supply,* p. 148.
13. Pitkin, *A Statistical View,* p. 98.
14. John G. Clark, *The Grain Trade in the Old Northwest* (Urbana and London: University of Illinois Press, 1966), p. 34. New Orleans of course was, and remained until the mid-1840s a major center of the coasting trade by which western produce was shipped to domestic markets on the eastern seaboard, a traffic which is beyond the scope of this study.
15. *Ibid.,* pp. 34-35.
16. Worthy P. Sterns, "The Foreign Trade of the United States from 1820 to 1840," *The Journal of Political Economy,* VIII (December, 1899), p. 36.
17. Clark, *The Grain Trade,* pp. 5-6.
18. Stern, "The Foreign Trade," p. 43.
19. Edwards, "American Agriculture," p. 218.
20. Thomas D. Odle, "The American Grain Trade of the Great Lakes, 1825-1873," *Inland Seas,* VII (1952), pp. 238-239.
21. Edwards, "American Agriculture," p. 219.
22. Frederick Merk, "The British Corn Crisis and the Oregon Treaty," *Agricultural History,* Vol. 8, No. 3 (July, 1934), pp. 107-108.
23. Herbert J. Wunderlich, "Foreign Grain Trade of the United States 1835-1860," *Iowa Journal of History and Politics,* XXXIII (January, 1935), p. 54.
24. Stern, "The Foreign Trade," pp. 41-42.
25. Wunderlich, "Foreign Grain Trade," p. 52.
26. Clark, *The Grain Trade,* p. 174.
27. Charles B. Kuhlmann, *The Development of the Flour Milling Industry in the United States* (Boston and New York: Houghton Mifflin Company, 1929), p. 288.
28. Morton Rothstein, *American Wheat and the British Market, 1860-1905,* (Unpublished doctoral dissertation, Cornell University, 1960), pp. 73-74.
29. Joseph Dart, "The Grain Elevators of Buffalo," *Buffalo Historical Society Publications,* I (1879), pp. 391-404.

30. Odle, "The American Grain Trade," p. 191.
31. Wunderlich, "Foreign Grain Trade," p. 62.
32. Charles H. Evans, "Exports, Domestic and Foreign from the American Colonies to Great Britain, from 1697 to 1789, Inclusive. Exports, Domestic and Foreign from the United States to All Countries, from 1789 to 1883, Inclusive." *House Miscellaneous Documents,* 48 Cong. 1 Sess. No. 49, Part 2 (1884), Serial 7236, pp. 20-23, 113-116.
33. U. S. Patent Office, *Annual Report,* 1847, p. 12.
34. Merk, "The British Corn Crisis," p. 111.
35. Wunderlich, "Foreign Grain Trade," pp. 31-32.
36. Clark, *The Grain Trade,* pp. 237-238.
37. *Ibid.,* p. 259.
38. Baring Brothers and Co. to Grinnell, Minturn and Co. April 18, 1854. Quoted in Thomas P. Martin, "The Staff of Life in Diplomacy and Politics during the Early Eighteen-Fifties," *Agricultural History,* Vol. 18, No. 1 (January, 1944), p. 14.
39. Evans, "Exports, Domestic and Foreign," pp. 113, 115-116.
40. Martin, "The Staff of Life," pp. 10-15.
41. *Niles' National Register,* Vol. LXIX, p. 69.
42. Clark, *The Grain Trade,* p. 187.
43. Evans, "Exports Domestic and Foreign," pp. 20-22, 46-49, 114-116, 173, 175.
44. Columbus, Ohio, *Statesman,* April 1853. Quoted in Martin, "The Staff of Life," p. 2.

III

La Belle Epoque

Was Britain's need for American grain the determining factor in her ultimate decision not to recognize the Confederacy during the Civil War? This provocative question has been debated for many years by a number of historians, each adducing convincing arguments in support of his thesis, but without being able to present conclusive evidence one way or the other.[1] There can be little doubt, however, that England's dependence on the United States for a sizable percentage of her breadstuffs requirements was one factor in her continued neutrality, despite the South's strategy of prohibiting cotton exports and the resulting disruption of the British textile industry. In any event, while speculation on what might have been the consequences of British intervention in the Civil War lies beyond the scope of this study, it is proper to consider the role played by American grain exports during this crucial period.

By 1860 the Industrial Revolution had transformed Great Britain from a grain-exporting country into a major and regular grain importer, depending on foreign supplies for about one-fourth of the total quantity of wheat needed for her population of 20 million. Also by 1860 the United States, thanks to the combined effects of westward migration, transportation extension, and agricultural mechanization, was becoming an important producer and exporter of the major cereals. Production of wheat alone increased from 100 million bushels in 1849 to 173 million in 1859, of which the free states and territories produced 142 millions, or 82 percent. The expansionary cycle gained further momentum in 1860, which saw a bumper crop of wheat and corn in the West and eastern North-Central states, with Ohio, Minnesota and Wisconsin increasing their wheat production by 66 percent over the crop of 1859, and Ohio's corn crop rising by 32 percent.

With the outbreak of war and the closing of the Mississippi, southern purchases of western wheat, which had amounted to about 10 million bushels a year, came to an end. Luckily for American grain farmers, grain formerly going down the Mississippi River could now go eastward via canals, natural waterways, and some new east-west railroads; Great Britain was a ready customer, and in 1861 she imported from the United States almost 25 million bushels of wheat and 2.4 million barrels of flour, equal to another 10.9 million bushels of wheat. Most of the 4 million bushels of wheat exported from the United States to Canada also undoubtedly went on to England. Including shipments to all countries, therefore, the first year of the Civil War there were exports of about 50 million bushels of American wheat compared with 16 million in 1860. The export price of wheat, as a result of such demand, averaged $1.23 a bushel in 1861, up from an average of 98 cents in 1860.[2] During the same year, exports of corn jumped to almost 11 million bushels from 3.3 million in 1860, while another million bushels was exported in the form of corn meal.

Crops failed again in England and France in 1861 and 1862, while production of wheat in the loyal states and territories kept on increasing to 187 million bushels in 1862 and 191 million the following year. Accordingly, American exports rose further, reaching combined totals equivalent to 58 million bushels of wheat and flour and 20 million bushels of corn and corn meal in 1862, and 56 and 17 million respectively in 1863.

In the three-year period of 1861-63, the United States supplied almost 41 percent of Great Britain's imports of wheat and flour, and it is reasonable to infer that if England had recognized the Confederacy in order to relieve the cotton shortage for her mills, she would have risked war with the Union and a consequent food shortage for her entire population.[3]

It is a fact that recognition of the Confederacy was seriously considered, and that there was much agitation in England for and against it, with such leading figures as Bright and Cobden speaking out in favor of respecting the Union. In any event, by the summer of 1863 news of the federal victories at Vicksburg and Gettysburg made it clear to the British government that the Northern cause would eventually prevail, and the danger of British intervention in the Civil War was decisively removed.

While the British market was and remained the principal outlet for American grain, the increasing concentration in urban centers of millions of nonagricultural workers who somehow had to be fed, and the relatively low levels of American grain prices,

An eighteenth century engraving showing a farm's layout.
(Collections of the Library of Congress)

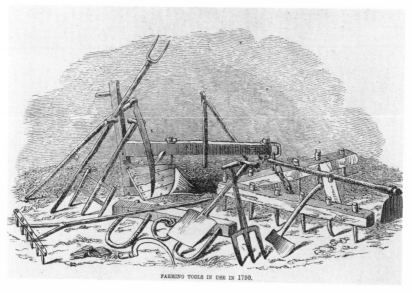

FARMING TOOLS IN USE IN 1790.

Farming Tools in use in 1790.
(The Smithsonian Institution)

Early silo design in the Columbian Magazine, 1786. The basic principles remain unchanged to this day.
(Collections of the Library of Congress)

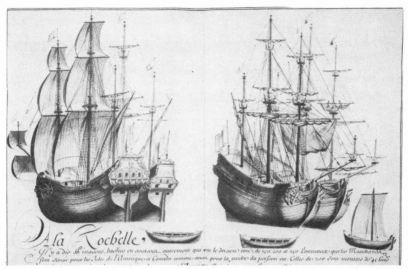

French *pinasses* of the seventeenth century. Ships such as these were used either for trading between the New World and France or for fishing. Engraved in 1679 by J. Jouve in *Desseins des differentes manieres de Vaisseaux que l'on voit . . . depuis Nantes jusqu'a Bayonne.*

(Musee de la Marine, Paris)

The Princess Royal, a big East Indiaman of the second half of the eighteenth century. Detail of a painting done in 1770 by J. Clevely the Elder

(National Maritime Museum, London)

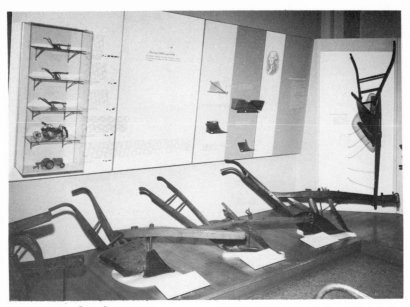

Early plows.
(The Smithsonian Institution)

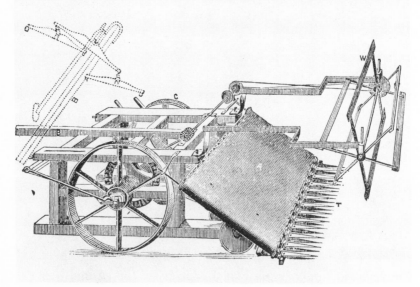

Bell's Reaping Machine, put in operation in 1828.
(The Smithsonian Institution)

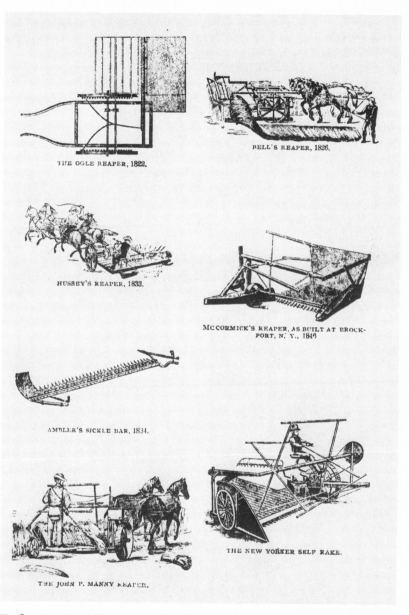

THE OGLE REAPER, 1822.

BELL'S REAPER, 1826.

HUSSEY'S REAPER, 1833.

MC CORMICK'S REAPER, AS BUILT AT BROCK-
PORT, N. Y., 1846

AMBLER'S SICKLE BAR, 1834.

THE NEW YORKER SELF RAKE.

THE JOHN P. MANNY REAPER.

Early nineteenth-century developments in agricultural machinery.

(The Smithsonian Institution)

A replica of Cyrus H. McCormick's first reaper (1831) in action.
(McCormick Collection, State Historical Society of Wisconsin)

A man harvesting wheat with a grain cradle.
(Caterpillar Tractor Company, Peoria, Illinois)

Grain cradlers harvesting a field of wheat, around the end of the nineteenth century.
(The International Harvester Collection, State Historical Society of Wisconsin)

The *Thetis*, a West Indiaman of the early nineteenth century. The vessel, with its fine lines and lofty rig, was lighter and faster than its relatives in the East India Service.
(Fifty Plates of Shipping and Craft, drawn and etched by E. W. Cooke, London: 1829)

A Prussian snow of the early nineteenth century. The vessel has the traditional lines of the merchantman built for capacity and not speed.
(*Fifty Plates of Shipping and Craft*, drawn and etched by E. W. Cooke, London: 1829)

A Ditching Plow. Detail of *Harper's Weekly* 1871 description of farming in Illinois.
(Collections of the Library of Congress)

PLANTING CORN.

Planting Corn. Detail of *Harper's Weekly* 1871 description of farming in Illinois.
(Collections of the Library of Congress)

CULTIVATING CORN.

Cultivating Corn. Detail of *Harper's Weekly* 1871 description of farming in Illinois.
(Collections of the Library of Congress)

Hedge Gang. Detail of *Harper's Weekly* 1871 description of farming in Illinois.
(Collections of the Library of Congress)

Mechanized threshing, using a true source of horsepower.
(Collections of the Library of Congress)

John Fitch's Steam-boat.
(South Street Seaport Museum, New York)

Robert Fulton's namesake, built in 1815.
(South Street Seaport Museum, New York)

The "James Monroe", first transatlantic liner to sail on schedule,
leaving South Street, January 5, 1818. The Black Ball Line's ships
left Liverpool on the 1st and New York on the 5th of each month,
beginning in January of 1818. If necessary, they would sail with
holds less than full and use steam tows to get to sea on time
against foul winds. Painting by George Campbell.
(South Street Seaport Museum, New York)

The Farmers' Movement in the West—Meeting of the Grangers
in the woods near Winchester, Scott County, Illinois, 1873.
(Collections of the Library of Congress)

An 1875 lithograph extolled the farmer's role.
(Collections of the Library of Congress)

Wheat Farming in California. Wood engravings in *The Graphic*,
1883.
(Collections of the Library of Congress)

Farming scene in *Leslie's News*, 1891.
(Collections of the Library of Congress)

Combines in the fields, ca. 1890.
(The International Harvester Collection, State Historical Society
of Wisconsin)

Farmers breaking sod in North Dakota.
(Albertype Collection, State Historical Society of Wisconsin)

made a growing number of other foreign countries look to the United States as a chief source of foodstuffs in the decades following the Civil War.

Before going on to examine the course of grain exports in the postwar period, however, it is necessary to dwell briefly on the extension of cultivation and the new production and marketing techniques whose development was indeed essentially responsible for the trade's enormous expansion.

First, the improvements in transportation and the declining cost of reaching the seaboard and overseas markets caused a continuing shift in the centers of grain production. The census of 1850 showed Pennsylvania, Ohio, New York and Virginia as the four principal wheat-growing states, accounting for 54 percent of the crop. In the same year the six Southern states of Tennessee, Kentucky, Virginia, North Carolina, Alabama and Georgia produced one-half of the country's corn crop, while the North Central states of Ohio, Indiana, and Illinois contributed only 22 percent. Ten years later, Illinois, Indiana, Wisconsin and Ohio occupied the top four places among wheat producers, followed by Virginia and Pennsylvania. In corn production the shift was equally dramatic, with the share of the three North Central states rising to 32 percent and that of the Southern ones falling to 27 percent.[4]

Then the westward movement received renewed momentum from the passage of the Homestead Act in 1862 and from the construction of transcontinental railroad lines. The act, which offered 160 acres of the public domain to any American who would cultivate the land for five years, or pay $1.25 an acre for it after residing on it for six months, attracted countless settlers to the territories between the Missouri River and the Pacific Ocean. The railroads, in turn, which between 1862 and 1871 were granted 125 million acres of public lands, resold much of their acreage to cattlemen and farmers. The construction of the Union Pacific Railroad in 1864-69 caused the extermination of the buffalo on the prairies and permitted the opening of the Great Plains to cultivation. The Morrill Act in 1862, establishing land-grant colleges, made many more millions of acres available to settlement and cultivation. Consequently, the centers of production shifted still further west.

By 1879, Iowa, Missouri, Kansas and Nebraska led in corn production with more than one-third of the total. In wheat, the leaders were still Illinois and Indiana, followed by Ohio and Michigan, with almost 40 percent of the total, but the next ranks were now occupied by the trans-Mississippi states, Minnesota (7.53%), Iowa (6.78%), Missouri (5.43%) and Kansas (3.77%). Pennsylvania, New York, and Virginia, which only forty years earlier had accounted for more than 40 percent of American wheat production, were now no longer significant producers.[5]

Also of paramount importance in this expansionary process was the emergence of California as a primary producer of wheat for export. Many of the forty-niners, once they recovered from the gold fever, turned to farming. The favorable climate helped them turn the Sacramento and San Joaquin valleys into veritable bonanzas by growing wheat on vast acreage with the widespread use of harvesting machinery, and the major portion of the crop was from the beginning intended to be exported, since California grain was found to be so hard and dry that it could withstand the long voyage around Cape Horn to Europe without spoiling. Most of this grain was carried in sailing vessels especially built for this trade after 1860 by Maine shipyards, the famous "down-easters" which combined the speed of the old China Clippers with bigger cargo capacity and smaller crews.

From the East Coast, instead, grain was now carried by both tramp sailing ships and by steamers. The latter, in fact, were eager to transport parcels of grain which provided an ideal ballast, and they often offered space at rates lower than those demanded by a sailing vessel for a full cargo.

Thus, during the two decades following the Civil War, the westward movement and the expansion of merchant shipping provided the basis for a tremendous rise in agricultural production and exports.

With regard to cultivation methods, although the beginning of widespread adoption of mechanized equipment by grain farmers came in the 1850s, the Civil War provided the decisive impulse towards farm mechanization. More than a million farmers donned blue uniforms, and the men and women who remained on the farms of the North and West had to resort more and more to machines in order to maintain and expand production as required by the exigencies of the war. The McCormick harvester, since its first invention in 1831 and its further improvement in 1847, had gained wide acceptance and had been followed by the development of many other mechanical implements for plowing, cultivating, reaping, and threshing. By the end of the war, the advantages of labor-saving devices had been amply demonstrated, and farmers engaged in commercial agriculture had come to consider farm machines as necessary implements.

Notable changes in grain transportation also occurred at this time. Throughout the 1850s railroad traffic had been hampered by the absence of through-freight arrangements between the eastern and western railroads, due principally to differences in track gauges and the resulting need to transship the grain and flour from one car to another. During the Civil War, however, the Baltimore & Ohio and the Pennsylvania Railroads, in order to better handle the very heavy traffic involved in the provisioning of the Union army, made through-freight agreements with a number of western railroads and embarked on a crash program of standardizing rail gauges. These agreements remained in force after the war, and with elimination of the need for breaking bulk it was possible to reduce freight rates. In the postwar period other eastern roads, such as the Vermont Central, the New York & Erie, and the New York Central, also reached through-freight agreements with several western lines. It was these through-freight arrangements which, in conjunction with the telegraph, permitted the movement of grain and flour directly from the production areas of the West to the consumption and export centers of the East.[6]

Through rail service, of course, did not fully develop until the 1880s, and in the meantime lake navigation continued to be a vital outlet for the movement of grain to seaboard. As a result, Chicago, because its location made it an ideal collecting, storing, marketing, and transfer center, became the focal point of the American grain trade during the years immediately preceding and following the Civil War.

It was at Chicago that the system of commingled storage of grain and the consequent issuance of warehouse receipts was first developed, with the attending standardization of inspections and grades.

Interestingly enough, the reason that these developments occurred first at Chicago lies in the unit size and number of the conveyances carrying grain to the Lake Michigan port. While lake and canal boats reaching Buffalo, Oswego, or New York, contained six to ten thousand bushels or more, the tens of thousands of railroad cars converging each year on Chicago held only three-

or four-hundred bushels. It was therefore essential to construct large storage facilities, to unload cars with utmost speed, and to fill the storage to capacity. The latter goal involved dumping in a common bin the grain belonging to different shippers, and it was thus necessary to establish a grading system which would allow an acceptable level of uniformity to be maintained. The subsequent issuance of warehouse receipts based on a definite quantity and grade rather than on an individual lot in store had two vital consequences. It created a new trade language, easily and generally understood by buyers and sellers, providing a common basis for comparing values and a better method of establishing prices. It also allowed trading to proceed quickly and in any volume on the floor of a board of trade or exchange, simply by the transfer of the receipts.[7]

Characteristic of this period was the rise and expansion of associations of grain dealers in the principal trading centers. There had been associations of merchants in the main American seaports since the early eighteenth century, but they had included members of all fields of business. By the middle of the nineteenth century, however, the increasing size and complexity of the grain trade prompted the organization of separate associations whose primary purpose was to safeguard the interests of the grain trade. The initiative for the organization of the Chicago Board of Trade in 1848 came from the town's grain merchants, although businessmen in other fields of commerce were also admitted to membership. The same can be said for the St. Louis Merchants' Exchange, organized in 1849. In New York as late as 1852 members of the grain trade, similarly to the traders in securities, did business on the curb at Broad and South Street, but during that year they formed the New York Corn Exchange, which eventually became the New York Produce Exchange. Two years later, the Corn Exchange Association was organized at Philadelphia. Other exchanges, aiming at standardizing and regulating the grain trade, as well as mediating disputes between members, came into being at this time in most major trading centers in the interior as well as at seaboard.[8]

The establishment of the elevator system and grading procedures, which gained quick and early acceptance in the interior grain centers, did not immediately extend to the seaboard export points. The first large elevator on the Atlantic was built at Portland, Maine, by the Grand Trunk Railway of Canada, but it was not until after 1865 that similar facilities were erected at Boston, Philadelphia, and Baltimore by the railroads serving those ports. Soon thereafter, the local grain exchanges instituted inspection and grading procedures. On the other hand, in New York, where most of the exporters were located, there was considerable resistance to change. This resistance was caused by a number of factors. First, a large percentage of the grain coming to New York was still being carried through the Erie Canal and kept in the canal boats until transferred to ocean-going vessels by means of floating elevators. These elevators and boat fleets represented very substantial investments which the owners naturally sought to protect. Second, there was the desire on the part of many firms which were simply branches of foreign importers to preserve the identity of superior lots of grain intended for shipment to their principals overseas. Also to be considered was the opposition of the boatmen, dockers and weighers, who saw in the proposed innovations a threat to their livelihood.

This struggle extended over an entire decade, pitting many members of the New York Produce Exchange against each other, and causing acrimonious controversies between grain merchants and representatives of the railroads.

As time progressed and the volume of grain carried to New York by railroads increased, the situation worsened. Each boxcar held only three- to four-hundred bushels, while trading in the New York Produce Exchange was carried out in multiples of eight thousand bushels, so that each delivery required the marshaling of a large number of individual railcars. These cars, once spotted in the yards on the New Jersey side of the Hudson, had to be unloaded into barges, which carried the grain to Brooklyn for further transfer to warehouses or directly to ships, and receivers were often negligent or tardy in calling for their goods with their own barges. Such was the resulting confusion in the yards that the railroads often preferred to discharge the cars and lighter the grain at their own expense in order to speed up the process. Finally, under pressure by the railroads and faced with the prospect of trade being diverted to other ports, the New York Produce Exchange in 1874 agreed to establish a uniform system of inspection and grading, so that commingled storage and faster handling could be achieved in the large elevators subsequently built by the railroads. The rail lines, in return, agreed to continue to provide free lighterage for export grain.

With the introduction of the telegraph and the transatlantic cable, as well as the establishment of uniform standards, a fundamental change also took place in the selling terms of domestic and export grain. Whereas most of the business had been done on a consignment basis in the past, with many middlemen and merchants acting as selling agents for the shippers in return for a commission, after the 1860s merchants increasingly began acting as principals. This was possible since they could now keep posted of market changes without delay and take prompt action in consequence of price fluctuations, knowing reasonably well what quality they would receive.

The largest concentration of export firms, whether purely American companies or resident agents for foreign importers, was to be found in New York. The choice of New York as headquarters by the principal exporters was not affected by the fact that after the 1860s, corn and flour were exported primarily from other ports such as Baltimore, Philadelphia, and Boston, and that much wheat was also diverted to those ports thanks to differential railroad freight rates favoring them over New York. In fact, the New York firms themselves were often instrumental in promoting movement through other ports in order to benefit from transportation advantages. There were at New York two main types of companies involved in grain exports. The "fobbers," as the name implies, were exclusively engaged in procuring grain from the West and selling round lots F.O.B. (free on board), loaded on the vessels presented by exporters who sold it overseas. Many other firms, instead, made sales abroad of grain bought directly in the interior as well as parcels bought from the "fobbers." Very often they could ship the grain on a through bill of lading from the Midwest all the way to the foreign destination. The "fobbers" were exclusively American firms, among whom the best known in this period were David Dows & Co., John B. Truesdell & Co., and Yale Kneeland. In the period following the Civil War and for several decades thereafter, many of the "pure" exporters were owned and managed by Englishmen connected with importers in Great Britain.

In 1863 a prominent Liverpool firm, Patterson Brothers, opened a New York branch managed by J. P. Preston, who in later years set up his own business. David Bingham, who settled in the United States in 1866, came from a family of Liverpool grain merchants, and soon became a major power in the New York market and within the New York Produce Exchange. Samuel Sanday, also from Liverpool, opened an office in New York in 1871 as agent for a British importer, and in 1880 established the company which during and after World War I was to become the principal English-owned grain company in America. Many other foreign firms, such as Sawyer, Wallice & Co. of London, Fowler Bros., Ltd., of Liverpool and Buenos Aires, Dreyfus et Cie. of Paris, and Ralli Brothers of London also operated in the grain export trade in New York. Among the principal American grain firms in New York were Busk & Jevons, J. W. Simon & Son, E. R. Livermore, J. H. Herrick, and Wyld & Marshall. Other prominent exporters in other cities were Gill & Fisher in Philadelphia, Nye Jenks & Co. in Baltimore, Balfour, Guthrie & Co. on the West Coast, and William T. Baker & Co. and Bartlett, Frazier & Co. in Chicago.[9] At this time, it should be noted, because of the nature of their business, grain export firms were relatively small in size as far as staffs and physical facilities were concerned.

Hand in hand with the development of instantaneous communications, grade standardization, and the growth of the exchanges, was the establishment within the exchanges themselves of futures markets, which operated side by side with the markets for cash grain. With this development, it became possible for exporters to conclude transactions for distant delivery without having to run undue market risks. When selling abroad, they could buy simultaneously an equivalent quantity of grain represented, not by an actual lot already harvested and in store which would have been costly to carry, but by the contractual obligation of the "futures" seller to deliver the grain at the agreed time. Conversely, the exporter who had acquired grain in anticipation of prompt sales which failed to materialize, or simply in order to have adequate stocks to fill expected future demand, could limit his risk of market loss by selling it in the "futures" market for later delivery. With the market risk thus reduced by "hedging," the difference between the prices paid to the farmers and the prices quoted abroad could be narrowed, providing benefits for all participants in the transaction and supplying stimulus to further expansion of grain exports.

Much has been written about the activities of the speculators who, in the days before government regulation, made the grain trading pits their hunting grounds and earned notoriety, opprobrium, and occasionally large profits through "squeezes" and "corners." Undoubtedly there were many abuses, some of which could be and were corrected by the exchanges themselves through revision of their rules, while others had to wait for federal intervention through the creation of supervisory agencies. Nevertheless, grain speculators as a group performed a vital function from the beginning by providing a counterpart to the hedging activities of merchants, millers, processors, and exporters.

Thanks to the combination of fast communications, large storage facilities, and futures trading, American exporters gradually became able to carry forward large surpluses when prices overseas were low, and could draw on these stocks when foreign markets rallied. In contrast, the annual volume of exports of the other major grain exporting countries was generally related almost exclusively to the size of the harvest rather than to the prices obtainable abroad.

Turning once more to a chronological review of grain exports during the last third of the nineteenth century, a graphic representation shows that, due in part to declining production caused by wartime disruption and postwar readjustment, exports of wheat and flour declined sharply after 1863, falling in 1867 to 10 million bushels, or a mere 20 percent of the wartime high level. Corn and corn meal, on the other hand, touched bottom earlier, and by 1867 had bounced back to an export volume of 16 million bushels. In 1866, incidentally, corn exports for the very first time exceeded exports of wheat and flour, European demand being stimulated by the Italo-Prussian War against Austria. After 1867 the course of exports of these two principal grains diverged once more, with wheat and flour in 1870 reaching the proportions of the 1863 peak, while corn and meal during the same year slumped to almost negligible levels.

The next decade saw an unprecedented surge in production and exports, amply fulfilling the most optimistic hopes of farmers and merchants, and the earlier enthusiasm of Anthony Trollope, who, after visiting Chicago and Buffalo in 1861, had written:

> . . . I went down to the granaries and climbed up into the elevators. I saw the wheat running in rivers from one vessel into another, and from the railroad vans up into the large bins on the top stories of the warehouses—for these rivers of food run up hill as easily as they go down. I saw the corn measured by the forty-bushel measure with as much ease as we measure

an ounce of cheese and with greater rapidity. I ascertained that the work week went on week-day and Sunday, day and night, incessantly—rivers of wheat and rivers of maize ever running. I saw the men bathed in corn, as they distributed it in its flow. I saw bins by the score laden with wheat, in each of which bins there was space for a comfortable residence. I breathed the flour and drank the flour and felt myself to be enveloped in a world of breadstuff. And then I believed, understood, and brought it home to myself as a fact that here in the corn lands of Michigan, and amid the bluffs of Wisconsin, and on the high table plains of Minnesota, and the prairies of Illinois had God prepared the food for the increasing millions of the Eastern world as also for the coming millions of the Western. . . . [10]

Combined exports of wheat and flour rose from 50 million bushels in 1871 to 175 million in 1880, while corn exports skyrocketed during the same years from 8 million to 116 million bushels.

One primary cause for the expansion of American grain exports in this period was the decline of Russia as an exporting country. This decline was caused by the unsettled conditions of her agriculture after emancipation of the serfs in 1861, and by her embroilment in war with Turkey in 1878. As a result, the normally importing countries of Western Europe turned increasingly to the United States for their supplies of breadstuffs. The Netherlands, for instance, which in 1870 had imported from America only seventy-one thousand bushels of wheat and 14,500 barrels of flour, in 1874 took 3.2 million bushels and 26,500 barrels respectively. Belgium's imports of American wheat and flour rose from 196,000 bushels and fifteen thousand barrels in 1870 to 3.7 million bushels and 72,500 barrels. By far the largest customer for American grain was, of course, still Great Britain, which throughout this decade took from 60 to 80 percent of total American wheat exports, the peak percentage being touched in 1875 when the United States shipped to Great Britain 42 million bushels of wheat out of a total exported of 53 million.[11] Well could a British journalist write in 1878 that "The United States, in consequence of the enormous increase of its cultivated area, following the development of its railroads, is now regarded as the controlling power of the corn markets of the world." [12]

Then came disastrous crop failures in England and Western Europe in 1879, 1880, and 1881. France, which heretofore had been only a marginal buyer of American wheat, imported from the United States 42 million bushels in 1879, 43 million the following year, and almost 30 million in 1881, while British imports for the same three years rose to 79, 82.5 and 65 million bushels respectively. Altogether, exports of wheat during these three crucial years accounted for almost one-third of total production.[13]

Because of drastic changes in trading patterns and foreign demand, the foreign market for American flour did not expand proportionately, even though exports of wheat were thus dramatically increasing.

Until the Civil War, most of the wheat had been exported in the form of flour in barrels. In the 1860s, however, European millers, especially in France, Hungary, and Germany, improved the milling process and produced flour which, although more expensive, was of decidedly higher grade and could therefore successfully compete with the American product in those markets, such as Great Britain and Brazil, where quality was more important than price.

The Hungarian process, which produced the highest grade of flour, consisted of grinding hard Danubian wheat between a series of porcelain rollers. By contrast, American millers were still employing millstones exclusively, and their flour, especially when made from spring wheat, had a coarse texture and a relatively dark color. Furthermore, American railroads favored wheat over flour by lower export rates, and import tariffs abroad were generally unfavorable to American flour.

As a result, while as late as 1870 more than 40 percent of American wheat exports had been made in the form of flour, the share of flour fell to 27 percent of the total in the five-year period ending in 1875, and to less than 19 percent five years later.[14]

The European need for grain during the critical period of scarcity in 1878-1881 was also reflected in the growth of corn exports. Although the corn crop had always been larger than that of wheat, since colonial times corn exports had generally been limited to relatively near destinations such as the West Indies, Cuba, Mexico, and Canada. This was due in part to the peculiarities of the grain, which tended to absorb atmospheric moisture and become "heated" during long sea voyages, and also to an ingrained prejudice on the part of the masses in much of Europe against the use of corn for human consumption. When, for instance, the British government had imported American corn meal into Ireland during the famine of 1846, the populace had thought it to be poisonous and had quickly dubbed it "Peel's brimstone." The serving of corn meal in Irish workhouses had actually led to riots.[15]

For many years after the Civil War the situation had remained the same as that outlined in 1855 by an American official, who, in reviewing the prospects for exporting corn, wrote:

> The admission here made that maize . . . is generally less relished than wheat, will doubtless be excepted to . . . but the writer is speaking of corn and wheat as they are presented in commerce in the cities on the Atlantic and Gulf of Mexico, and not as in the home consumption of the people of the corn-growing regions. . . . To them it is at once the great staple of life and among the most relishable article of aliment. But it is otherwise in the cities, where such skill and facilities are not possessed; and it is far otherwise in the countries of Europe where many of the people are not even yet convinced that a palatable bread may be made from the flour of maize. Thus we find that, although cheap bread is, as has been said, the great want of Europe, the Indian corn exported from the United States is even yet far less in value than the wheat exported. . . . [16]

With improved methods of handling and drying the grain, and the growing use of steamers instead of sailing vessels, the first obstacle to transatlantic corn exports was removed; sheer necessity, in turn, made corn more palatable to many Europeans, while corn also began to be used there for livestock feeding; consequently, corn exports in 1880 were twenty times what they had been in 1870. Although they did not again surpass the 100 million bushel mark until fifteen years later, corn exports after 1880 remained substantial, even if still small compared with total production and domestic usage.

From the standpoint of price, the decade of the seventies was one of relative stability. The export price of wheat was $1.32 a bushel in 1871 and $1.25 a bushel in 1880. Corn fluctuated somewhat more widely, from 76 cents to 54 cents a bushel, the lower price undoubtedly contributing to the record exports of 1880.[17]

In contrast, the decade which began in 1881 was characterized by sharply fluctuating but generally downward-trending grain prices, as a result of increasing competition in world markets. In the early 1880s Russia reappeared as a major wheat exporter, so much so that by 1888 and until 1890 she supplied more wheat to the British market than did the United States. English public opinion, which had heretofore willingly accepted the unrestricted flow of American grain to the British Isles despite the fact that the American tariff effectively kept out many British products, began clamoring for the development of substitute sources of supply within the Empire. Wheat production was actively subsidized in Canada, Australia and especially India, and by the mid-1880s India had become a major exporter of wheat. From 1881 to 1890, therefore, American exports of wheat declined, falling from 150 million bushels to 54 million, although in the intervening years exports of about 100 million bushels a year were registered for 1882, 1883, and 1887. Corn exports also declined, and fluctuated even more than those of wheat, with the high for the decade being reached in 1881 at 75 million bushels, and the lows at 16 million bushels occurring in 1882 and 1890.[18]

A bright feature in the picture during this period was the renewed expansion of flour exports. Superior European milling technology had put American flour at a disadvantage after the Civil War. Furthermore, exporters generally assembled lots produced by many different mills into a single shipment, so that as late as 1879 The London Miller, while praising the fact that American flour was now at last being shipped in space-saving bags, could comment: "The qualities of the flour are very various and the brands legion . . . . One important fact in favor of the English miller is that the American maker has yet to learn that the bakers here expect, above all things, uniformity." [19]

In the 1870s, however, a veritable revolution in American milling methods had taken place, with the introduction of chilled steel rollers and a "middling purifier" which produced a flour fully comparable to that produced in Hungary with porcelain rollers.

Furthermore, many of the larger mills in Minneapolis, New York, Buffalo, St. Louis, and Kansas City proceeded to establish direct connections with buyers in the United Kingdom and on the Continent, assuring such buyers of consistently high-grade and uniform supplies. As a result, exports of flour rose from less than 7 million barrels in 1881 to more than 13 million ten years later, and climbed further during the next decade, with annual average exports of 16 million barrels. In both 1899 and 1900, flour exports well exceeded 18 million barrels, or the equivalent of about 84 million bushels of wheat. Consequently, the percentage of wheat exported as flour, which had fallen to less than 19 percent by 1880, rose again appreciably and averaged more than 40 percent during the rest of the century.

The best known among these exporting mills, and the one which perhaps did most in promoting the expansion of American flour exports, was the Washburn-Crosby Company of Minneapolis, which was eventually to become the nucleus of General Mills.

If exports of flour were steadily on the increase during the last decade of the nineteenth century, the same could not be said for exports of wheat. The decade opened favorably, as a result of serious crop failures in India and Russia in both 1891 and 1892. Consequently, American exports during those years climbed back to 129 and 125 million bushels, and receded slightly to 108 million in 1893. There seemed to be justification, therefore, for the boast of an American trade writer who in 1892 had thus chided Great Britain:

> ... Once India was the land of promised plenty, then Australia, then Russia, but the broad prairies of the United States still continue to supply Johnny Bull's right and tight little island with the major portion of the breadstuffs imported. England may as well accept the inevitable, for America is the granary of the importing world.[20]

The following three years, however, were marked by a world glut of unprecedented proportions, caused by perfect growing weather in all exporting countries and the emergence of Argentina as a major producer. Prices fell to the lowest levels of the century in 1895, with American wheat being sold at an average of 58 cents a bushel. Despite the low prices, American exports contracted sharply, falling that year to 75 million bushels. The last four years of the century witnessed a revival of wheat exports, with volume exceeding 100 million bushels each year and coming close to 150 million in 1898. In that year, thanks to the increased flour exports mentioned above, combined American exports of wheat and flour reached an all-time high of 224 million bushels. The 200 million bushel mark was also exceeded that year and the following one by exports of corn, which in the last decade of the century moved abroad in consistently increasing volume.

The last decade of the nineteenth century, distinguished by striking increases in global population which naturally expanded the demand for breadgrains, also saw a manifold expansion in exports of other grains. Oats, especially, which in previous years had been exported in quantities varying from a few hundred thousand bushels to 3 or 4 million bushels, spurted in 1896 to 30 million and to 52 million the following year, remaining at well over 30 million for the rest of the period. The growth in demand arose primarily from the feeding needs of expanded numbers of draft animals.

Exports of barley, used primarily for brewing, rose in comparable proportions during the last five years of the century, averaging about 15 million bushels a year. Rye, still strictly a breadgrain, did not show a similarly sustained increase, but exports of this grain did reach 12 million bushels in 1892, 10 million in 1897, and almost 16 million in 1898.[21]

Both rice and flaxseed during this period were not significant export items. As to rice, a main cause may be found in the disruption of southern agriculture. In 1860 and 1861 respectively 81 million and 40 million pounds of this grain had been exported. For the rest of the century, however, exports never exceeded 3 or 4 million pounds a year, and during many years they were indeed negligible. As to flaxseed, which continued to be the principal oilseed, the growing need of oils for domestic consumption precluded exports and in fact caused sizable importation to take place.

As could be expected, the phenomenal growth of American grain trading did not escape attention in the age of "muckraking." Forty years after Trollope had rhapsodized on the magnitude of Chicago's oceans of golden grain, the purple prose of Frank Norris dealt in The Octopus with "the war between the [California] wheat grower and the Railroad Trust"[22] and in The Pit with an attempted corner in wheat on the Chicago Board of Trade.

Wrote Norris in describing the tumultuous effects of incoming harvest on the unsuccessful speculator:

> . . . The eddies were gathering; the thousands of subsidiary torrents that fed the cloaca were moving. From all over the immediate neighborhood they came, from the offices of hun-

dreds of commission houses, from brokers' offices, from banks,
. . . And even from greater distances they came; auxiliary cur-
rents set in from all the reach of the great Northwest, from
Minneapolis, Duluth, and Milwaukee . . . The Atlantic Seaboard, New York, and Boston and Philadelphia sent out their
tributary streams; London, Liverpool, Paris, and Odessa merged
their influences with the vast world-wide flowing that bore
down upon Chicago, and that now began slowly, slowly to
centre and circle about the Wheat Pit of the Board of Trade . . .
It was the Wheat, the Wheat! It was on the move again.
From the farms of Illinois and Iowa, from the ranches of
Kansas and Nebraska, from all the reaches of the Middle West,
the Wheat, like a tidal wave, was rising, rising . . . What were
these shouting, gesticulating men of the Board of Trade, these
brokers, traders, and speculators? It was not these he fought,
it was that fatal New Harvest; it was the Wheat. . . . What
were those scattered hundreds of farmers of the Middle West,
who because he had put the price so high had planted the grain
as never before? What had they to do with it? Why the Wheat
had grown itself; demand and supply, these were the two great
laws the Wheat obeyed. Almost blasphemous in his effrontery,
he had tampered with these laws, and had roused a Titan. . . .
The new harvest was coming in; the new harvest of wheat,
huge beyond possibility of control; so vast that no money
could buy it, so swift that no strategy could turn it. . . .[23]

Norris' words, written in 1900, echoed the recent burgeoning
of populist sentiment pitting the agrarian West and South against
the moneyed East, condemning imperialism, and advocating free
coinage of silver. Nineteen-hundred was the year in which William McKinley and William Jennings Bryan competed for the
presidency a second time. It was also the year which brought to
a close the first full century of America's life as a nation and also
the period which marked her emergence as the world's leader
in agricultural production and exports. From now on, American
farmers and businessmen, as well as government officials, would
have to combine their efforts to try to maintain such leadership
in an increasingly troubled world.

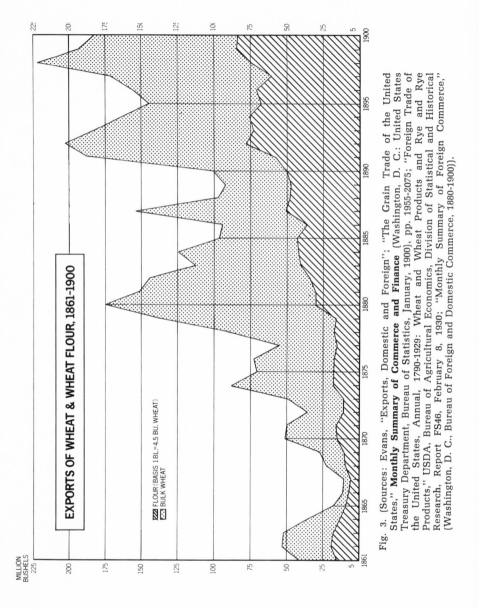

Fig. 3. (Sources: Evans, "Exports, Domestic and Foreign"; "The Grain Trade of the United States," **Monthly Summary of Commerce and Finance** (Washington, D. C.: United States Treasury Department, Bureau of Statistics, January, 1900), pp. 1955-2075; "Foreign Trade of the United States, Annual, 1790-1929: Wheat and Wheat Products and Rye and Rye Products," USDA, Bureau of Agricultural Economics, Division of Statistical and Historical Research, Report FS46, February 8, 1930; "Monthly Summary of Foreign Commerce," (Washington, D. C., Bureau of Foreign and Domestic Commerce, 1880-1900)).

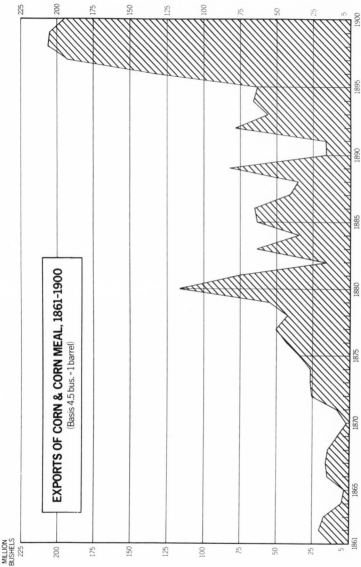

MILLION BUSHELS

EXPORTS OF CORN & CORN MEAL, 1861-1900

(Basis 4.5 bus. = 1 barrel)

Fig. 4. (Sources: Evans, "Exports, Domestic and Foreign"; "The Grain Trade of the United States," Monthly Summary of Commerce and Finance (Washington, D. C.: United States Treasury Department, Bureau of Statistics, January, 1900), pp. 1955-2075; "Foreign Trade of the United States, Annual, 1790-1929: Wheat and Wheat Products and Rye and Rye Products," USDA, Bureau of Agricultural Economics, Division of Statistical and Historical Research, Report FS46, February 8, 1930; "Monthly Summary of Foreign Commerce," (Washington, D. C., Bureau of Foreign and Domestic Commerce, 1880-1900)).

Table 5—Total Exports of Wheat and Flour, 1867-1900

(000 omitted)

Year	Bulk Wheat (bus.)	Wheat Flour (brls.)	Grain Equiv. of Flour (bus.)	Total (bus.)
1861	26,594	3,410	15,345.0	41,939.0
1862	34,069	4,308	19,386.0	53,455.0
1863	35,210	3,929	17,680.5	52,890.5
1864	21,898	3,079	13,855.5	35,753.5
1865	8,549	2,187	9,841.5	18,390.5
1866	3,272	1,657	7,456.5	10,728.5
1867	4,267	1,312	5,904.0	10,171.0
1868	14,517	2,007	9,031.5	23,548.5
1869	16,537	2,355	10,597.5	27,134.5
1870	36,145	3,396	15,282.0	51,427.0
1871	34,074	3,624	16,308.0	50,382.0
1872	25,453	2,427	10,921.5	36,374.5
1873	38,114	2,518	11,331.0	49,445.0
1874	70,188	4,046	18,207.0	88,395.0
1875	53,024	3,964	17,838.0	70,862.0
1876	54,873	3,927	17,671.5	72,544.0
1877	40,461	3,337	15,016.5	55,477.0
1878	72,304	3,945	17,752.5	90,056.0
1879	122,133	3,624	16,308.0	138,441.0
1880	144,483	6,828	30,726.0	175,209.0
1881	120,463	6,827	30,721.5	151,184.0
1882	110,343	7,587	34,141.5	144,484.0
1883	71,013	9,243	41,593.5	112,606.0
1884	81,628	9,526	42,867.0	124,495.0
1885	53,025	9,616	43,272.0	96,297.0
1886	57,759	8,179	36,805.5	94,564.0
1887	101,972	11,518	51,831.0	153,803.0
1888	49,532	10,715	48,217.5	97,749.0
1889	45,611	10,451	47,029.5	92,640.0
1890	49,271	11,319	50,935.5	100,206.0
1891	129,639	13,024	58,608.0	188,247.0
1892	125,518	17,409	78,340.5	203,858.0
1893	108,402	16,417	73,876.5	182,278.0
1894	87,450	16,859	75,865.5	163,315.0
1895	75,222	15,267	68,701.5	143,923.0
1896	83,756	15,856	71,352.0	155,108.0
1897	109,909	13,596	61,182.0	171,091.0
1898	149,246	16,570	74,565.0	223,811.0
1899	109,635	18,717	84,226.5	193,861.0
1900	99,079	18,633	83,848.5	182,927.0

Table 6—Total Exports of Corn and Corn Meal, 1861-1900

(000 omitted)

Year	Bulk Corn (bus.)	Corn Meal (brls.)	Grain Equiv. of Meal (bus.)	Total (bus.)
1861	10,678	203	913.5	11,591.5
1862	18,905	254	1,143.0	20,048.0
1863	16,119	258	1,161.0	17,280.0
1864	4,097	262	1,179.0	5,276.0
1865	2,818	199	895.5	3,713.5
1866	13,517	237	1,066.5	14,583.5
1867	14,890	284	1,278.0	16,168.0
1868	13,094	337	1,516.5	14,610.5
1869	6,821	310	1,395.0	8,216.0
1870	1,288	187	841.5	2,129.5
1871	7,459	212	954.0	8,413.0
1872	23,984	309	1,390.5	25,374.5
1873	24,770	403	1,813.5	26,583.5
1874	24,457	388	1,746.0	26,203.0
1875	33,265	292	1,314.0	34,579.0
1876	41,621	354	1,593.0	43,214.0
1877	48,030	448	2,016.0	50,046.0
1878	40,655	433	1,948.5	42,603.5
1879	53,298	397	1,786.5	55,084.5
1880	114,279	387	1,741.5	116,020.5
1881	72,826	405	1,822.5	74,648.5
1882	15,424	239	1,075.5	16,499.5
1883	61,275	486	2,187.0	63,462.0
1884	32,989	240	1,080.0	34,069.0
1885	62,526	305	1,372.5	63,898.5
1886	63,655	250	1,125.0	64,780.0
1887	40,307	250	1,125.0	41,432.0
1888	33,773	285	1,282.5	35,055.5
1889	81,278	331	1,489.5	82,767.5
1890	14,725	352	1,584.0	16,309.0
1891	15,172	274	1,233.0	16,405.0
1892	77,471	200	900.0	78,371.0
1893	55,144	200	900.0	56,044.0
1894	65,000	300	1,350.0	66,350.0
1895	61,956	264	1,188.0	63,144.0
1896	131,961	301	1,354.5	133,315.5
1897	189,128	718	3,231.0	192,359.0
1898	207,309	854	3,843.0	211,152.0
1899	206,135	869	3,910.5	210,045.5
1900	190,386	861	3,874.5	194,260.5

Table 7—Average Export Prices of Wheat, Flour, Corn and Corn Meal, 1861-1900

Year	Wheat ($ per bus.)	Wheat Flour ($ per brl.)	Corn (¢ per bus.)	Corn Meal ($ per brl.)
1861	1.23	5.70	.64	3.44
1862	1.14	5.64	.55	3.07
1863	1.29	6.46	.66	3.93
1864	1.33	7.19	.82	5.14
1865	1.95	10.41	1.31	7.47
1866	1.41	8.43	.82	4.76
1867	1.27	9.85	1.00	5.47
1868	1.90	10.06	1.17	6.15
1869	1.39	7.74	.97	5.34
1870	1.29	6.11	.92	5.00
1871	1.32	6.59	.76	4.49
1872	1.47	7.14	.69	3.93
1873	1.31	7.56	.62	3.65
1874	1.43	7.56	.71	3.94
1875	1.12	5.97	.85	4.42
1876	1.24	6.21	.67	3.68
1877	1.17	6.48	.59	3.37
1878	1.34	6.36	.56	3.08
1879	1.07	5.25	.47	2.65
1880	1.24	5.88	.54	2.80
1881	1.11	5.67	.55	2.92
1882	1.19	6.15	.67	4.34
1883	1.13	5.96	.68	3.67
1884	1.07	5.59	.60	3.24
1885	.86	4.90	.53	3.03
1886	.87	4.70	.50	2.80
1887	.89	4.51	.48	2.70
1888	.85	4.58	.55	2.91
1889	.90	4.83	.44	2.62
1890	.83	4.66	.43	2.61
1891	.93	4.82	.65	3.34
1892	1.03	4.96	.53	3.00
1893	.80	4.54	.49	2.90
1894	.67	4.11	.47	2.64
1895	.58	3.38	.45	2.64
1896	.65	3.56	.33	2.11
1897	.75	3.84	.32	1.95
1898	.98	4.51	.37	2.21
1899	.75	3.95	.40	2.27
1900	.72	3.62	.44	2.30

Table 8—Total Exports of Barley, Oats and Rye, 1861-1900

(000 omitted)

Year	Barley (bus.)	Oats (bus.)	Rye (bus.)
1861	...	...	...
1862	...	...	...
1863	...	...	...
1864	66	306	155
1865	67	332	134
1866	...	1,246	417
1867	...	826	147
1868	10	123	501
1869	59	482	50
1870	255	122	158
1871	340	148	50
1872	87	263	795
1873	482	714	562
1874	320	813	1,564
1875	91	505	207
1876	318	1,406	544
1877	1,186	2,854	2,189
1878	3,922	3,715	4,208
1879	716	5,452	4,852
1880	1,248	592	2,353
1881	227	604	985
1882	313	524	1,421
1883	424	486	4,690
1884	991	3,249	5,234
1885	250	7,330	745
1886	301	1,328	217
1887	1,349	776	377
1888	1,566	523	163
1889	1,071	2,529	1,046
1890	828	12,207	1,719
1891	2,585	4,973	7,956
1892	2,893	4,414	12,069
1893	3,139	6,807	1,494
1894	5,301	398	249
1895	3,540	2,039	...
1896	16,668	30,517	5,323
1897	15,927	52,319	10,583
1898	4,541	49,930	15,719
1899	16,942	41,085	4,852
1900	12,319	32,183	1,997

Notes To Chapter III

1. Louis Bernard Schmidt, "The Influence of Wheat and Cotton on Anglo-American Relations during the Civil War," *Iowa Journal of History and Politics,* XVI (July, 1918), pp. 400-439. Eli Ginzberg, "The Economics of British Neutrality during the Civil War," *Agricultural History,* X (October, 1936), pp. 147-156. Robert H. Jones, "Long Live the King?", *Agricultural History,* Vol. 37 No. 3 (July, 1963), pp. 166-169.

2. Paul W. Gates, *Agriculture and the Civil War* (New York: Alfred A. Knopf, 1965), pp. 224-228.

3. Schmidt, "The Influence of Wheat and Cotton," pp. 429-431.

4. "The Grain Trade of the United States," *Monthly Summary of Commerce and Finance* (Washington, D. C.: United States Treasury Department, Bureau of Statistics, January, 1900), p. 1991.

5. *Ibid.*

6. Odle, "The American Grain Trade," pp. 257-259.

7. H. Bruce Price, "Grain Standardization," *American Economic Review,* II (June, 1921), p. 227. Guy A. Lee, "The Historical Significance of the Chicago Grain Elevator System," *Agricultural History,* Vol. 11 No. 1 (Jan. 1937), pp. 21-23.

8. Rothstein, *American Wheat,* pp. 85-88.

9. *Ibid.,* pp. 258-273.

10. Anthony Trollope, *North America* (London: 1862), I, pp. 231-232.

11. "The Grain Trade of the United States," p. 2024.

12. The Saturday Review (London), reprinted in *The Northwestern Miller,* October 4, 1878, quoted in Rothstein, p. 213.

13."The Grain Trade of the United States," p. 2024.

14. Kuhlmann, *The Development of the Flour Milling Industry,* p. 288.

15. Merk, "The British Corn Crisis," p. 99.

16. U. S. Patent Office, *Annual Report,* Agriculture, (Washington, D.C.: 1855), p. 157.

17. "The Grain Trade of the United States," p. 2024.

18. *Ibid.*

19. Reprinted in *The Northwestern Miller,* June 20, 1879, quoted in Kuhlmann, p. 291.

20. *American Elevator and Grain Trade,* November 15, 1892, quoted in Rothstein, p. 235.

21. "Monthly Summary of Foreign Commerce," (Washington, D.C., Bureau of Foreign and Domestic Commerce, 1880-1900) *passim.*

22. Frank Norris, *The Pit,* (New York: Grove Press, Inc., 1956), p. viii.

23. *Ibid.,* p. 380, pp. 373-374.

IV

Feasts, Famines, and World Wars

The last third of the nineteenth century had represented a "golden age" for American grain exports, and the opening years of the twentieth seemed to portend a continuation of high volume shipments to a wide and growing range of destinations. The United Kingdom was still the leading buyer of American grain, in 1901 taking 87 million bushels of wheat and 10 million barrels of flour out of 179 million bushels and 18 million barrels exported. Caused in part by the spurt of neocolonialism which characterized the early 1900s, the roster of countries importing significant quantities of American grain, mainly consisting in the past of European and Central American nations, was by now expanded to include many African and Asian destinations. Hong Kong, for instance, after 1897 and until World War I, received an average of more than one million barrels of American flour each year. The Chinese Empire was a substantial buyer of flour, as were Japan and Brazil. The British colonies in Africa took a sizable volume of wheat and corn as well as flour.

The early 1900s also brought about notable developments in both the geographical distribution of shipping points and the structure of the grain trade.

New Orleans, which until 1890 had accounted for a mere 5 percent of wheat exports from Atlantic and Gulf ports, had doubled its share by 1900. Even more spectacular was the growth of Galveston, which, thanks to the expansion of rail connections and of wheat cultivation into Oklahoma and North Texas, by 1900 accounted for more than 15 percent of the foreign trade in wheat east of the Rockies. The expansion of Gulf ports resulted in the organization in April, 1900, of the Gulf Ports Grain Exporters' Association, which, as the North American Export Grain Association, continues to this day to·represent the grain trade in dealing with foreign associations. Also by 1904 Boston had passed New York in volume of wheat exports, and Montreal was emerging as an important competitor. On the West Coast, Portland was replacing the California ports as the main export outlet for grain.

As to the complexion of the trade, the trend was increasingly towards concentration. Success in the foreign wheat trade rested to a large extent on the ability to obtain favorable inland freight rates, and such rates could be achieved only by those who shipped the grain in large lots. Grain merchants in the interior also found it more difficult to obtain favorable rates for ocean freight.[1] As a result, and also because of the large amount of capital required, the export grain trade was handled by a relatively limited number of large concerns. These firms, in their efforts to buy at the lowest levels in order to compete in the world market, acquired and operated terminal elevators and lines of country elevators in the producing areas. In addition, they opened networks of trading offices in all major grain centers. Samuel Sanday & Co., Louis Dreyfus & Co., Bartlett, Frazier & Co., and Balfour, Guthrie were still most active, and their ranks were joined by newer firms such as J. Rosenbaum & Co., Norris Grain Co., and Charles Counselman in Chicago, A. J. Sawyer in Minneapolis, and the Hall-Baker Grain Co. in Kansas City and New York. Hedging techniques were by now quite sophisticated, and use of the future markets permitted the exporters to operate in increasingly large volume without incurring prohibitive risks. Speculation was, of course, also widespread, but more on the part of local traders than of the large export houses.

American grain exports continued high in 1902 and 1903. Poor harvests in 1904 and 1905 caused exports to drop sharply, but the contraction had only a limited and temporary effect on the generally healthy conditions of American agriculture.

This was indeed a time of prosperity such as the American farmers had never known before. Prices of farm products were continually rising, registering an increase of 52 percent from 1900 to 1910. Land values were also moving sharply upwards. In 1910 the value of farms in South Dakota was four times what it had been in 1900. During the same decade, farm lands in Iowa and Minnesota more than doubled in value.[2] And, most important, the prices of what the farmer had to sell kept abreast with those of what he had to buy, so that when, in later and leaner years, a formula was sought to recreate a "normal" relationship between farm and nonfarm prices, 1909-1914 was selected as the ideal "parity" period.

There were numerous causes for this prosperity. Increased use of fertilizers brought greater yields and facilitated the continuing shift to commercial agriculture and the utilization of marginal lands. Scientific advances in seed selection and the development of improved varieties also progressed rapidly at this time. The U. S. Department of Agriculture, which had been created as a bureau by President Lincoln in 1862 and had been given cabinet status in 1889, began to take an increasingly active part in bringing a more enlightened and scientific atmosphere to the nation's agriculture. In addition, the farmers' dependence on foreign markets for their surplus production appeared to diminish as domestic consumption, spurred by the great waves of immigration during the previous decades and by the continuing trend to industrialization and urbanization, absorbed a growing share of the nation's harvests.

This relative prosperity was, of course, not immune to problems, many of them arising from the growing complexity of transportation and marketing of farm products. The agrarian discontent which in the last decades of the nineteenth century had found its expression in the activities of the Farmers Alliance, the National Grange of the Patrons of Husbandry, and the Populist party, and which had failed to achieve significant gains after the turn of the century, caused the emergence of the Farmers Union and of the American Society of Equity, both organized in 1902. Main targets of these fast growing and aggressive organizations were discriminatory railroad rates, alleged or actual abuses by middlemen, elevator operators, and speculators, tariff discrimination, monopolistic practices, and deflationary credit policies. One way in which farmers sought to achieve more advantageous returns for their roles as producers was the organization of specialized business cooperatives, but the principal direction of their quest for improvements was pressure for governmental intervention and regulatory legislation.

With the sudden ascent of Theodore Roosevelt to the presidency, many of the farmers' demands received prompt and concrete satisfaction. The Elkins Act in 1903 outlawed rebates by the railroads to large shippers and compelled them to charge published rates without discrimination. This act corrected many of the weaknesses of the Interstate Commerce Act of 1887, which had been unable to cope with the burgeoning concentration of power of the large railroad systems. The Elkins Act was followed in 1906 by the Hepburn Bill, which gave the Interstate Commerce Commission full authority to regulate railroad rates. Theodore Roosevelt's relentless drive towards forest conservation and land reclamation is too well known to need more than passing mention, and the implementation of his policies in these fields produced inestimable benefits for American agriculture. Similarly beneficial was passage of the Food and Drug Act and of the Meat Inspection Act in 1906. And in 1908 Roosevelt appointed a commission on country life, whose report the following year registered alarm at the continuing population shift away from farming, and encouraged the growth of the farm cooperative movement.

Roosevelt's "trustbusting" and conservationist campaigns were followed even more vigorously by his successor, William Howard Taft, but it fell to the Democratic administration of Woodrow Wilson to carry forward a program of reforms, many of which directly or indirectly greatly affected grain production and trade. "We have," Wilson said in his first inaugural address, "a body of agricultural activities never yet given the efficiency of great business undertakings or served as it should be through the instrumentality of science taken directly to the farm, or afforded the facilities of credit best suited to its practical needs. . . ." [3]

To remedy this situation, Wilson's "New Freedom" program included the passage in 1914 of the Smith-Lever Act, providing cooperative agricultural extension work, followed in 1917 by the Smith-Hughes Act authorizing federal grants for teaching of agriculture in high schools. The Federal Reserve Banking Act of 1913 was supplemented three years later by the Federal Farm Loan Act. Among the first objects of investigation by the Federal Trade Commission after its creation in September of 1914 were the "Packer Trust," the "Harvester Trust," and the Corn Products Refining Company. In the same year, the Clayton Antitrust Act sought to clarify and strengthen the provisions of the Sherman Act of 1891. Two laws of greatest significance for the grain trade were the Grain Standards Act and the Warehouse Act, both passed in August, 1916. The former sought to eliminate unfair trading practices by empowering the secretary of agriculture to establish uniform standards of quality for grain moving in interstate commerce. The latter aimed at facilitating more orderly marketing of farm products by providing storage to alleviate seasonal gluts. Trading in futures was regulated for cotton by an act passed in 1914, but grain futures were still free of government regulations and would remain so for eight more years.

Those were crucial years for the grain trade, marked by a war of unparalleled magnitude, famines and relief efforts of enormous scope, and, ultimately, the beginning of a long period of agricultural depression.

The years 1904 and 1905 had seen a sharp reduction in overseas shipments of American grains, due to the combination of poor harvests and increased domestic demand. In the years that followed, combined volume of wheat and flour exports fluctuated appreciably, from highs of about 150 million bushels in 1907, 1908, and 1913, to lows of 60 and 80 million in 1910 and 1911. Corn exports, which had exceeded 100 million bushels in 1901 and again in 1905 and 1906, seesawed even more sharply, falling to below 20 million bushels in 1902 and again in 1914.

With the increasing competition from other sources of supply, such as Australia, Argentina, Russia, and Canada, which were in their turn assuming the role of surplus producer earlier held by the United States, the world was no longer primarily dependent on the United States for its grain imports. In addition, the growth of nationalism in Europe and the resulting stiffening of protective tariff barriers placed further obstacles in the path of American grain exports. As a result, agricultural exports, which had in the past always constituted the major portion of American foreign trade, and which as late as 1900 had still accounted for 61.6 percent of the total, declined both in absolute and relative importance.[4]

The outbreak of World War I in July, 1914, brought a dramatic change in this picture. England could no longer count on continental sources for supplies of breadstuffs, and in the first months of the war France lost control of the areas that normally produced much of her grain. Wheat, of course, has always occupied a most important place among war materials because of its special qualities, being nutritious, nonperishable, easily handled, and universally accepted as food. Both governments from the outset made heavy purchases in the United States through the intermediary of private firms, with the result that American exports of wheat and flour in 1914 once more exceeded 200 million bushels. Spurred by such increased demand, American farmers the following year raised wheat acreage from 53.5 million to more than 60 million acres, which, coupled with the highest yield on record of 17 bushels per acre, resulted in a record wheat crop of over one billion bushels in 1915. Exports continued at a high level, with total 1915 shipments of more than 275 million bushels of wheat and flour, as well as 50 million bushels of corn, 26 million bushels of barley, and over 100 million bushels of oats.

Meanwhile, in the summer and fall of 1914 a fortuitous set of circumstances first brought into public service a man whose views and activities were to be of paramount importance for the grain trade throughout the war years and for much of the postwar period. Herbert Hoover, a wealthy mining engineer with vast international experience, happened to be in London when war was declared, and, at the request of the American ambassador, he brilliantly organized the repatriation of more than 100,000 American tourists left stranded by the onset of hostilities. When the German armies overran most of Belgium and parts of northern France, confiscating food supplies with the result that the civilian population of more than ten million faced virtual starvation, Hoover also accepted the chairmanship of a relief commission which organized the purchasing, shipping, and handling of food supplies for the occupied regions.

The Commission for the Relief of Belgium, under Hoover's management, bought wheat abroad and shipped it to Belgium where it was resold to the millers at cost. The flour was then sold to the bakers, and the bread to the populace, always at the combined cost of raw materials plus labor. The price of Belgian wheat was also controlled by requiring that grain dealers in the country sell their wheat at fixed prices to certain licensed middlemen in the cities.[5]

The experience gained by Hoover in managing grain prices in Belgium was to be applied by him when, following the United States entry into the war in April, 1917, he was appointed Food Administrator, and he quickly established a system of controls which successfully managed pricing and distribution, and, indirectly, production of grain and other foodstuffs. Until then, however, no controls of any kind had existed, and their absence was felt in sharply rising prices when poor harvests in 1916 and 1917 brought forth wheat crops of only about 600 million bushels. In October, 1916, Great Britain established the Royal Wheat Commission, which was to buy, sell, and distribute all wheat and flour in the United Kingdom, and one month later, to better coordinate their purchasing efforts, the British, French and Italian governments signed the Wheat Executive Agreement. This agreement provided that the three countries pool their grain requirements as well as their shipping tonnage and entrusted the Royal Wheat Commission with the actual purchasing of wheat and flour for the combine.

In the United States the Allies' purchases were handled by the Wheat Export Company at 27 Beaver Street in New York. "In reality, the W(heat) E(xport) C(ompany) was Samuel Sanday & Company, the largest English grain exporter in the United States; the Royal Wheat Commission preferred to work under such a cover in order not to irritate Americans by the picture of open buying by the British government." [6]

That there was cause for more than irritation on the part of the American populace was amply shown by the steep rises in prices of foodstuffs. Minneapolis flour prices went from $6.66 a barrel in 1915 to $11.34 in early 1917, and by May were at $17.80 a barrel. No. 2 red winter wheat, which had gone from $1.15 bushel to $1.88 between July and November, 1916, reached $3.25 early in May of 1917. On May 11 the price hit $3.45 in Chicago, partly as a result of an involuntary corner by the Wheat Export Company which, unable to accumulate forward stocks of cash grain because of a scarcity of foreign exchange, had been buying May futures through the early months of 1917.[7] Between July, 1916, and April, 1917, food prices in the United States increased by 46 percent on an average, and in February, 1917, food riots spread through many eastern cities.

This was the situation which confronted Hoover when he returned to the United States in May, 1917, and was asked by President Wilson to organize the United States Food Administration.

Hoover's activities in this task are documented in detail in the second of his four volumes entitled *An American Epic,* as well as in a large number of monographs published by his principal assistants. For the purposes of this study, it is sufficient to note that, archaic as his social philosophy may have been, Hoover was indeed an organizing genius, and his management of grain supplies, prices, and distribution during World War I achieved the seemingly contradictory goals of securing adequate prices for grain producers while safeguarding accessible prices for consumers.

On August 10, 1917, President Wilson signed the Food Control Act which established a guaranteed price of $2.00 a bushel for wheat of the 1918 crop. Two days later Herbert Hoover announced that, in order to eliminate speculation in wheat and flour, all elevators and mills with over 100 barrels of daily capacity would be required to obtain a government license. Under the terms of the license only reasonable and customary charges would be made for warehousing and no wheat could be stored for more than thirty days without government approval. The grain exchanges would have to suspend all dealings and quotations in wheat futures.

> In substitution of the broken-down marketing machinery, (Hoover stated) the Food Administration proposes to open agencies for the purchase of all wheat at the principal terminals, carrying on its transactions with the usual dealers and is prepared to take the whole harvest, if necessary, in order to maintain a fair price, and will resell wheat for export in such quantities as we can afford to part with in protection of our own people on one hand and to sell on the other to the millers for domestic consumption.[8]

A few days later, by Wilson's executive order, the Food Administration Grain Corporation came into being, with a capital of $50 million and a staff of experienced grain traders, headed by Julius Barnes of New York. The country was divided by the Grain Corporation into fourteen zones, consisting of the principal terminal and seaboard markets along with their naturally tributary territories; purchasing agents were placed by the Grain Corporation in each of the zones. Thus, the Grain Corporation became the virtual arbiter, not only of grain distribution in the United States, but also of the supplies available for the sustenance of the Allied populations and armies in Europe. The price for the 1917 wheat crop was fixed by President Wilson at $2.20 a bushel.

From September to December, 1917, combined American exports of wheat and flour averaged 15 million bushels a month, but during the remainder of the crop year they dropped to approximately 10 to 12 million bushels monthly.[9]

The magnitude of the American effort in supplying the Allies with breadstuffs can best be realized from the fact that by the end of the crop year in June, 1918, the total carryover of wheat in the entire country was a mere 17 million bushels. It is a measure of Hoover's and Barnes' brilliant managerial ability that they succeeded in maintaining stable prices and distribution despite the barely adequate supply. Nevertheless, as has been aptly stated:

> Wheat price management during 1917-1918 depended on the exercise of power outside the market. Herbert Hoover managed wheat prices during 1917-1918 because he controlled the supply. Such control involved not only the Grain Corporation's own purchases, but control over the country and mill elevators, and this was the result of intense bargaining between Hoover and businessmen. Managing the supply also depended on Hoover's power to regulate the flow of exports and imports. Hoover achieved such power by adroit use of the embargo laws, by exploiting the financial exhaustion of the Allies, and by crude threats to shut the Allies out of the American market.[10]

The next crop year, however, confronted Hoover and Barnes with entirely different problems, caused by a bumper harvest of more than 900 million bushels of wheat. Corn, being in short supply because of the scarcity of seed, was exported in 1918 and 1919 in relatively reduced volume. However, a 300 million bushel surplus of wheat, which the Grain Corporation stood committed to buy in any amount at the statutory $2.00 a bushel, threatened to cause the financial collapse of the Corporation and, in turn, that of the American wheat market. Through protracted negotiations, Hoover and Barnes obtained from the Allies a commitment to prepurchase a "reserve" quantity of 100 million bushels, with the price to be fixed after monthly negotiations and with storage charges absorbed by the buyers. Shortly afterwards, the end of the war in November, 1918, again raised doubts about the Grain Corporation's ability to sustain export volume and wheat prices, all of which to a large extent depended on whether the United States would continue to extend loans to the Allies for the purchase of grain, and whether the Allies would turn again to cheaper if more distant sources of supply. Many months of active bargaining followed, but in the end, due primarily to British inability to shift the bulk of their purchases to Australia through lack of shipping, the Allies did take as much grain as Hoover and Barnes wanted to ship them. Altogether, more than 267 million bushels of wheat and flour were exported from the United States in 1919.

American farmers, still acting as if the war's demands would continue indefinitely, planted 76 million acres to wheat for the 1919 crop, and once more harvested close to a billion bushels. Circumstances had changed, however. Government price guarantees, set at $2.26 a bushel, came to an end in May, 1920. Food controls had been lifted in December, 1918, and the United States Grain Corporation which, still under the direction of Julius Barnes, had succeeded at that time the Food Administration Grain Corporation, also ceased its operations at the end of May, 1920. On July 15, the commodity exchanges resumed trading in grain futures. The grain trade was thus again free to operate according to the law of supply and demand, and, as a result, a rude awakening was in store for American farmers.

The war had apparently been a period of farm prosperity, with gross farm income rising from about $7.5 billion in 1910-1914 to $17.7 billion in 1919,[11] and the value of all farm lands and buildings going from $35 billion in 1910 to $66 billion in 1920.[12]

The price of wheat had risen sharply in the spring of 1920, going from $2.30 a bushel for No. 2 wheat at Chicago in November to as high as $2.97 in May. This, however, was mainly due to breakdowns in transportation to distributing centers and to continuing foreign demand. "Prices in the terminal markets . . . reflected the shortage of grain urgently needed for immediate consumption and to apply on export contracts, and they did not reflect the supply situation back in the country." [13]

Grain exports continued high in 1920, with combined shipments of wheat and flour totaling more than 300 million bushels. Starting in June, 1920, however, prices began a decline which went on unchecked until by November, 1921, No. 2 wheat sold at $1.09 a bushel at Chicago.

The main cause of this precipitous price drop was the fundamental change which the war had brought about in the United States position in international trade. Prior to 1914, America had been a debtor nation, and could therefore export more than it imported without upsetting the international balance. But having become, as a result of the war, the world's largest creditor nation, she could maintain a high level of exports at satisfactory prices only by increasing the volume of imports or by extending additional loans. As wartime credits to the Allies were ended in June,

Corn harvest, Norton County, Kansas, in 1890.
(Kansas State Historical Society)

Plowing by oxen in Connecticut, 1899.
(Collections of the Library of Congress)

Evolution of the sickle and flail: 33 horses harvesting, cutting, threshing, and sacking wheat at Walla Walla, Washington, 1902. (Collections of the Library of Congress)

The Best combined harvester is shown in the fields in Washington state during harvest around 1900.
(Caterpillar Tractor Company, Peoria, Illinois)

The last word in big wheels! Built in 1900 by the Best Manufacturing Company for the Middle River Farming Company, Stockton, California, this tractor had wood covered drive wheels 15′ wide and 9′ in diameter. Total weight, 41 tons.
(Caterpillar Tractor Company, Peoria, Illinois)

Flying Cloud, which in 1854 established the record time of 89 days and 8 hours for the New York—San Francisco run.
(South Street Seaport Museum, New York)

The Clipper Ship *Sovereign of the Seas*, built in Donald Mc-
Kay's famous East Boston yard. She and her sister ships carried
grain from San Francisco to Liverpool in slightly over 100 days.
(South Street Seaport Museum, New York)

Fulwood of Liverpool, off cape Leeuwin, Australia, 15th Feb.
1895.
(Alexander Turnbull Library, Wellington, New Zealand)

Leviathan Clipper Ship, *The Great Republic*, fully rigged.
(South Street Seaport Museum, New York)

TOXTETH
(Historical Collection, Title Insurance & Trust Co., San Diego,
California)

Mississippi River landing in 1906.
(Collections of the Library of Congress)

Loading the great whaleback ship at the famous grain elevators,
Chicago, 1895.
(Collections of the Library of Congress)

Great Northern Elevator and shipping at Buffalo, N. Y. in 1900.
(Collections of the Library of Congress)

River and Elevators at Buffalo, N. Y. in 1900.
(Collections of the Library of Congress)

Shipping at Buffalo, N. Y. in 1908.
(Collections of the Library of Congress)

Marketing wheat in Mandan, North Dakota, in the early twentieth century.
(Collections of the Library of Congress)

A country elevator in 1911.
(Collections of the Library of Congress)

1924—Tyler, Kansas Country Elevator
(United States Department of Agriculture)

Oct. 1924—Montana—Hauling wheat to market. A ten horse team, hitched two abreast, hauling three wagons at one trip. A total of 300 bushels of wheat was hauled by this outfit, 100 bushels to a wagon.

(United States Department of Agriculture)

Nov. 1924—Montana—Motor trucks waiting to unload wheat at the elevator.

(United States Department of Agriculture)

1919—View of Erie Elevator, Jersey City. Loading vessels with grain.

(United States Department of Agriculture)

1924—Rail cars being brought across on a float from the railroad yards on the New Jersey side to the railroad Pier 21 in New York.

(United States Department of Agriculture)

1920's—Duluth, Minesota—Grain elevator & ship loading.
(United States Department of Agriculture)

1923—Buffalo—Unloading a vessel at the Frontier Elevator of
the Washburn Crosby Company.
(United States Department of Agriculture)

Rice threshing in Texas.
Albertype Collection, State Historical Society of Wisconsin)

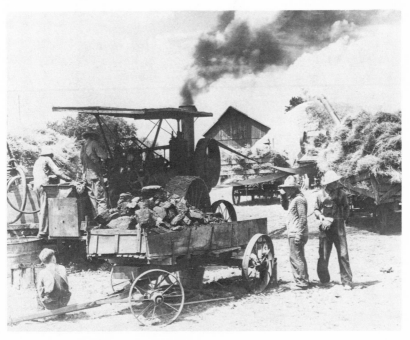

Coal Burning Thresher, 1934.
(J. W. McManigal Agricultural Photographs, Horton, Kansas)

The *Thomas W. Lawson*, a steel-hulled seven-masted cargo sailing ship.

Oregon, 1939—Barges on Columbia River, arriving at Terminal
Elevator with sacked wheat.
(United States Department of Agriculture)

Preparing land in Montgomery County, Maryland, to be seeded
to winter wheat in 1941.
(United States Department of Agriculture)

Eighteen miles west of Pendleton, Oregon, a farmer is seeding
winter wheat in 1946.
(United States Department of Agriculture)

Combining wheat in a Kansas field near Hayes in July, 1941.
(United States Department of Agriculture)

1919, and a strong protectionist trend opposed import expansion, foreign countries, although desperately needing grain, lacked the means to buy at the prices of the war period. Since the American farmer, however, had overexpanded production far in excess of domestic needs, the surplus had to be exported, and it could be shipped abroad only at the prices foreign buyers were willing and able to pay. After all, as the *1920 Yearbook* of the U. S. Department of Agriculture pointed out:

> . . . the prices of agricultural products are controlled by a world price level in which the supply and demand for a particular commodity is reflected in the price not alone at the place where the demand is strongest but in other producing and consuming centers as well.
>
> This is particularly true in the case of grain, where we have a price level with its base at Liverpool, which is the highest price-level point, becoming lower as you approach the producing center. The difference between the two points represents the cost of transportation and handling. If any wheat port on the Atlantic, the Baltic Sea, or the Mediterranean gets out of line 3 or 4 cents on the price of wheat, within 24 hours or less cargoes will be diverted to that port by wireless.[14]

Indeed, as grain prices broke in the United States after June, 1920, a rapid price decline followed throughout the world. "In the Fall of 1920, wheat was imported into Liverpool from Manchuria at lower prices than from the United States or Canada, while early in 1921, wheat could be purchased more cheaply in Argentina, Australia, India, and Manchuria than in Canada or this country." [15]

In the face of increasing competition from other world producers, American farmers in 1921 brought in another bumper grain crop, and total exports hit new highs, reaching that year over 350 million bushels of wheat and flour, 57 million of rye, and almost 130 million bushels of corn. Prices, however, were in many cases lower than cost of production. Illinois corn, which in 1919 had sold at $1.30 a bushel, by late 1921 had declined to 38 cents,[16] and in the winter of 1921 Nebraska farmers were burning corn for fuel.[17]

A problem of such magnitude could only be solved by government intervention, but the Republican administration of Warren

G. Harding, in which Herbert Hoover had become secretary of commerce, was not ready to consider any of the steps which would be part of the "New Deal" a decade later. Hoover had, soon after the armistice, organized the allocation of relief supplies throughout Europe, and, through the distribution of American grain and other foodstuffs, had managed to feed millions of children as well as adults in many parts of the continent emerging from five years of conflict. That he used his control over food relief as a weapon to try to stem the "red tide" in Central Europe and Russia does not change the fact that relief was received and famines averted or mitigated, thanks primarily to American grain exports. But Hoover's laissez-faire philosophy pitted him firmly in opposition to peacetime government interference with what he considered immutable economic laws, and thus put him at odds with Secretary of Agriculture Henry C. Wallace, who was trying to combine a scientific outlook with a practical approach in solving the many problems confronting American farmers.[18]

Wallace was indeed able to build up the scope and functions of the Department of Agriculture far beyond its previous activities, but he did not have the presidential ear and the support of big business as did Herbert Hoover. As a result, throughout the administrations of Harding and Coolidge, Hoover exerted considerable influence, which influence was instrumental in preventing enactment of measures designed to foster agricultural exports.

There was no shortage of such proposed measures. In May, 1921, Sen. George Norris of Nebraska had introduced a bill which would have set up a government corporation to buy farm products for cash and sell them abroad on credit, but at Hoover's instigation the measure was replaced by a revival and an extension of the powers of the War Finance Corporation. The next year the Ladd-Sinclair bill would have extended the life of the U. S. Grain Corporation, now being liquidated, until 1927, with a direction to buy farm products at prices remunerative to the producers and to sell them abroad at world prices. The Gooding bill would have formed a new government corporation to buy the 1923, 1924, and 1925 wheat crops at minimum prices, while the Little bill would have authorized the secretary of agriculture to buy and store grain to support prices.[19]

The flurry of legislative proposals at this time was stimulated by increasing agitation by the farmers' organizations, which now comprised, in addition to the Grange and the Farmers Union, the Non-Partisan League, which had arisen in 1915 as the most militant farm group, and the American Farm Bureau Federation, which had been organized in 1920. Under their pressure a number of senators and congressmen from agricultural states had joined in the so-called Farm Bloc, whose efforts did achieve some successes such as passage of the Emergency Agricultural Credits Act in August, 1921, and the Grain Futures Act in September, 1922. Congressional shortsightedness, in the same period, brought forth the Emergency Tariff Act in May, 1921, and the Fordney-McCumber Tariff in September of the following year, placing further obstacles in the path of potential foreign customers for American products. With continuing scarcity of foreign exchange, and in spite of abysmally low prices, overseas buyers were only able to purchase 164 million bushels of American wheat, and 15 million barrels of flour in 1922. Corn exports, thanks to the grain's cheapness, reached 163 million bushels.

The year 1922 saw the publication of a plan which was to constitute the basis for the proposals expanded during the following years in the five McNary-Haugen bills. Conceived by George N. Peek and Hugh S. Johnson, two officials of a plow factory in Moline, Illinois, who were understandably concerned with the inability of impoverished farmers to buy new implements, the plan was outlined in a pamphlet entitled *Equality for Agriculture*, and it clearly stated:

> The doctrine of protection must be revised to insure agriculture equality of tariff protection and a fair exchange value with other commodities, on the domestic market, or the protective principle must perish.
> It can be so revised only by some plan, in respect of surplus crops, to equalize supply with demand on the domestic market, at not to exceed fair exchange value with other commodities, to protect that value by a tariff, and to divert surplus to export and sell it at world price.[20]

The plan, as Peek and Johnson envisaged it, would automatically result in adjustment of production to combined domestic and foreign demand by requiring that losses incurred in the disposal of surpluses be borne by the surplus producers. "Any plan which would assess that loss against the nation," they wrote, "would encourage increased surplus, and consequent dissipation of national wealth on foreign shores." [21]

As the Peek-Johnson plan gained circulation and pressure for action mounted, Congress searched for some practical means of promoting farm exports. The Webb-Pomerene Act, exempting from antitrust regulations corporations organized exclusively to engage in the export trade, had been passed in 1918, and in February, 1922, the Capper-Volstead Act freed marketing cooperatives from the restrictions of the antitrust laws.

Between May, 1922, and June, 1923, the Senate received the reports of an investigation into the methods and operations of grain exporters by the Federal Trade Commission. The commission examined in detail the records of most of the largest exporters and came up with no startling findings or brilliant recommendations. It found, as was to be expected, that most of the grain export business was in the hands of a few large firms, that many of these were either branches of foreign importers or American companies wholly or partly foreign owned, and that many export firms also owned or controlled both country and terminal elevators. It determined that "the financial results of both exporters and fobbers during 1920 and 1921 varied from considerable losses to large profits" and that ". . . though a large part of the merchandising was hedged in the futures market . . . apparently speculative transactions in futures also occurred." [22] The commission's conclusions merely suggested certain changes in the rules of the Chicago Board of Trade and an increase in the construction of public elevators by railroads or government agencies.

The farm crisis continued through 1923, and grain exports were further sharply reduced. Bulk wheat, for which the farmer received an average of 92 cents a bushel, was down in export volume to 98 million bushels, but another 73 million bushels were exported in the form of flour. All other grain exports were also cut, corn down to 42 million bushels, and rye to 30 million. Altogether, exports of crude foodstuffs, principally grain, which had amounted to $673 million in 1921, fell to $257 million in 1923.

As has been acutely summarized, "(r)etrenchment, bankruptcy, and increased debt brought agriculture through to the end of a prolonged crisis period and into a clearer recognition that the crisis was but the beginning of a new farm problem," which was "a convergence of difficulties: high costs of production, burdensome distribution charges, production beyond domestic requirements, and low-level purchasing power of foreign markets." [23]

Although the crisis was over by the end of 1923, it was followed by a chronic agricultural depression which was to last until relieved by full-scale government intervention and the demands of a new wartime economy.

Meanwhile, efforts continued on the part of farm organizations and members of Congress to devise new schemes to raise prices and foster exports. These efforts, from 1924 to 1928, found expression in the series of bills introduced by Senator McNary of Oregon and Representative Haugen of Iowa. The basic principle of all five McNary-Haugen bills was the same: they proposed the setting up of a government export corporation, with a capital of $200 million, to buy farm products at so-called ratio-prices, that is, prices determined by the relationship of each commodity to the general price level of the prewar period. In the case of wheat, for example, which had sold at 98 cents a bushel before the war, when the general price index was at 100, and was selling at 92 cents in 1923, when the index was up to 156, the ratio price would have been 156 percent of 98 cents, or $1.53. Any quantities in excess of domestic needs would be sold by the corporation for export at world prices. The farmer would be paid partly in cash and partly in "scrip," which at year's end the corporation would redeem at whatever fraction of its face value remained after covering the losses incurred in the export sales.

The first three versions of the McNary-Haugen bill were defeated in Congress, and when the bill finally passed, in 1927 and again in 1928, it was vetoed by President Coolidge with the hearty blessing of Herbert Hoover, who favored instead a plan to assist and coordinate cooperative marketing. Despite its failure, however, the McNary-Haugen crusade was instrumental in promoting a changed attitude toward agriculture which was to have a much greater impact in the 1930s than it would have had in the 1920s.[24]

Another scheme to promote exports at this time was a proposal advanced by the Grange, known as the "Export Debenture Plan." Under this plan, exporters were to be given by the government debentures for the difference between domestic and world market prices. The exporter could sell the debentures at face value to an importer, who in turn could use them to pay custom duties; the exporter could thus afford to pay farmers the higher domestic price while selling overseas at world prices. This plan, too, came to nothing, owing, to a large extent, to Hoover's opposition both before and after he became president, and also to the fact that throughout the 1920s most people connected with the grain trade were violently opposed to surplus-control legislation.[25]

The course of grain exports during this period continued to fluctuate between highs of over 200 million bushels of wheat and flour in 1924 and 1927 and lows of under 150 million in 1925 and 1928. Corn exports remained very depressed throughout the period.

It thus fell to Herbert Hoover, soon after his election to the presidency by an overwhelming plurality in a period of unprecedented business prosperity, to redeem his campaign promises to take some action to help the more distressed segments of agriculture. This action took the form of the Agricultural Marketing Act of 1929, which created a farm board whose main functions were to be to minimize speculation, to promote the organization of cooperatives, to prevent inefficient methods of distribution, and to avoid or control surpluses. Before the board could begin to function, however, the onset of the Great Depression, epitomized by the stock market crash of October, 1929, made the crisis no longer an agricultural but a nationwide one.

In the pre-Keynesian economic climate of the times, President Hoover and the Seventy-first Congress could think of no better remedy than a strengthening of economic nationalism, embodied in July, 1930, in the Hawley-Smoot Tariff Act, which raised tariffs to all-time highs and effectively excluded most imports. The natural reaction of foreign countries was the erection of barriers against American products, emphasis on self-sufficiency through increased local cultivation, and expanded trade with competing grain producers such as Canada, Argentina, and Australia, whose costs of production were lower than those of American farmers, and which were willing to accept payment in manufactured goods. Eased by the blind expansion of economic protectionism, the tidal wave symbolized by Wall Street's Black Tuesday reached foreign shores, and by the spring of 1931 the Great Depression became worldwide.

The Farm Board, which in October, 1929, had set up the Farmers National Grain Corporation to regulate the activities of marketing cooperatives, in February, 1930, organized the Grain Stabilization Corporation, which tried to support the market by buying up surplus volume of wheat. With foreign markets glutted by bumper crops, American grain exports in 1930 and 1931 declined further, and by the end of June, 1931, the Farm Board owned 257 million bushels of wheat. At this point the board stopped trying to hold prices above the world market and began dumping its stocks with easily predictable results. Wheat prices on the farm, which in mid-June, 1931, had averaged 52 cents a bushel, by July 15 had fallen to 36 cents.[26] Trying to dispose of its wheat at any cost, the board donated 80 million bushels to the Red Cross for relief feeding, bartered 25 million bushels for Brazilian coffee, and even sold wheat to China and Germany in exchange for long-term bonds. Prices of other grains were equally depressed, while production remained at unjustifiably high levels in the face of sharply reduced demand. During the period 1929-1933 agricultural production declined only 6 percent, while agricultural commodity prices fell 63 percent. The production of agricultural implements dropped 80 percent, but prices declined only 6 percent. By February, 1933, farm commodities in general could purchase only half as much as in the period 1909-1914.[27]

The overproduction, despite the continuing decline in farm population, was basically due to the lack of alternatives for farmers, who felt that increasing the size of their harvests was the only way to get enough cash to stay afloat. This higher output came primarily from expanded acreage and from increased yields through wider use of fertilizers, farm machinery, and improved seeds. The tractor, which had come into general use in the 1920s, had replaced horses and mules which had previously consumed the products of 70 million acres of farmland, but these acres continued to be planted and harvested. The drastic curtailment of immigration initiated by Congress in 1924 had further limited the growth of domestic demand, and significant changes in eating habits also reduced consumption of certain crops.

There had been, in the 1920s, plans to control production, as opposed to the maintenance of a two-price system advocated by McNary-Haugenists. A U.S.D.A. economist, W. J. Spillman, had formulated a Domestic Allotment Plan in 1927, and two years later a similar plan had been presented to Congress by a group headed by Harvard economist John D. Black. A Voluntary Domestic Allotment Plan, the work of Professor Milburn Wilson of Montana, had subsequently gained wide circulation and had won the endorsement of many influential farm leaders and businessmen by the time the 1932 campaign pitted Herbert Hoover against Franklin Roosevelt. The summer of 1932 saw the outbreak of the short-lived but violent and headline-catching Farmers' Holiday led by Milo Reno, followed in the fall and winter by nationwide protest marches and by the meeting in Washington of the Farmers' National Relief Conference. This Conference in no uncertain terms demanded legislative action to stem the tide of farm foreclosures and to provide effective measures for the economic improvement of American agriculture.

The overwhelming victory of the Democrats at the polls was a most eloquent rejection by the American electorate of Hoover's laissez-faire philosophy, and it also proved "that the years of agitation had created general acceptance of the idea that the federal government had an obligation to do something—whatever it might be in specific detail—to improve farm conditions." [28] That "something" was passage of the Agricultural Adjustment Act in May of 1933, which act embodied many measures aimed at restoring a more stable climate for agricultural production and trade: liberalized farm credit, control of production, the establishment of standards of parity-prices, a "processing tax" to finance crop reduction, and the use of marketing agreements to stabilize prices and to subsidize exports.

To head the Department of Agriculture and implement the AAA, Franklin Roosevelt chose another of the Wallaces of Iowa, Henry A. Wallace, whose vision of the needs and potentials of American agriculture was no less than that of his father. The first results of the new law were gratifying for farmers. The 1933 wheat crop was less than 60 percent of that of 1931, and corn production was only four-fifths as large as in 1932, but farm prices, which in 1932 had stood at 55 percent of the 1909-1914 parity period, were up to 83 percent by July, 1933 and held at close to 80 percent for the rest of the year.

If the AAA's implementation was beneficial for farm prices, however, it was equally effective in reducing volume of exports, particularly grain. Some efforts were made to stimulate wheat exports from the Pacific Northwest by extending loans to China and to the Philippines, and for wheat and flour an Export Indemnity Program was instituted which was to last until the end of World War II, providing subsidies ranging from 6 to 61 cents a bushel to permit even the limited export volume of that period. In the aggregate, however, these efforts did not achieve significant results.

An attempt was also made by the United States and several

other countries to regulate world trade in wheat by signing an international wheat agreement in 1933. The agreement, however, broke down the following year. The Reciprocal Trade Agreement Act of 1934, renewed in 1937 and in 1940, was a significant step in the sensible direction of promoting trade expansion by lowering tariff barriers, but the enormous stocks in the surplus-producing areas and the continuing distress in most of the importing countries prevented any increase in the volume of grain exports. On the contrary, export volume decreased sharply and consistently, with corn falling to negligible proportions until 1938, and wheat exports also experiencing a similar contraction. As a result of droughts in 1934 and 1936, this period actually saw a substantial volume of wheat being imported for milling into the United States.

By 1937 it appeared that, even if grain exports were suffering, agriculture as a whole was well on the way to recovery. The Commodity Credit Corporation, which had been created in 1933 shortly after the abolition of Hoover's Farm Board, had successfully stabilized prices by making nonrecourse loans on basic farm products, helped in the domestic disposal of the grain so acquired by the droughts of 1934 and 1936. Other significant legislation affecting the agricultural production and trade had also been enacted, primarily the Soil Conservation and Domestic Allotment Act passed in February, 1936, to replace the AAA which had been crippled in January by the Supreme Court's decision in the Hoosac Mills Case, and the amendment and amplification a few months later of the Grain Futures Act with the resulting creation of the Commodity Exchange Commission under the Department of Agriculture.

In 1938, however, a new Agricultural Adjustment Act established higher "parity" levels at which CCC was directed to make nonrecourse loans to growers, and thus set the stage for a renewed accumulation of burdensome surpluses. Despite a sudden spurt in 1938 of corn exports to 151 million bushels, by October, 1939, corn stocks were at 550 million bushels, or more than twice the high carryovers of the 1920s. In the same year, although wheat and flour exports broke through the 100 million bushel level for the first time since 1931, stocks of wheat in CCC's hands also registered substantial increases.

Thanks to these abundant carryovers, the outbreak of World War II did not have a significant effect on American grain prices, which were in fact slightly lower in 1940 than they had averaged in 1935-1939. The next year, however, brought a price increase of nearly 25 percent, and farm production also rose by 13 percent over the earlier base period [29] in response, not only to price incentives, but also to technological innovations in farm machinery and seed varieties. By the summer of 1941, with passage of the Lend-Lease Act and the growing need to supply food to beleaguered England, efforts were being made by the Department of Agriculture to increase production of certain agricultural commodities. Wheat and corn were not among them, however, and in fact an appreciable reduction in wheat acreage was recommended as stocks were ample and the shortage of shipping gave preference to concentrated foods of high nutritive value rather than to wheat. In any event, Canada was the closer and more logical supplier of wheat to both England and Russia.

The Japanese attack on Pearl Harbor brought the American farmer closer to the battle line, and food production expanded in all sectors, including bread grains, feed grains, and especially oilseeds. In both 1942 and 1943, wheat carryovers exceeded 600 million bushels while corn stocks were well over 400 million.

The war period, which kept American grain exports to rather low levels, saw also a relative contraction in domestic demand, as war prosperity caused a shift in the eating habits of vast numbers of formerly low-income Americans, whose higher earnings allowed the purchase of more meat and less bread. The many attempts to control the consequent inflation and black markets resulted in the imposition of price ceilings and the subsidizing of many agricultural products at the processor and consumer levels, over the violent protests of the principal farm organizations.

That farmers had little reason to complain, however, is shown by the fact that while in 1939 the ratio of prices received by farmers to prices paid by them had stood at 77, by 1942 it had reached 106, and 119 by 1943, dropping back only slightly through the rest of the war years.[30] Furthermore, in order to stimulate production, Congress had guaranteed that farm support prices would be maintained at 90 percent of parity for two years after the end of the war. When the war ended, in the summer of 1945, the United States then had ample stocks of foodstuffs with which to supply the pressing needs of friends and former foes. What foreign nations lacked were the means of paying for their purchases: Britain, virtually bankrupted by the war, and no longer able to rely on Lend-Lease supplies, obtained from the United States a loan of $3.75 billion in 1946, but the rest of the former belligerents were not even in condition to negotiate loans with any hope of servicing or repayment.

The means to avert hunger and stagnation in the needy countries of the free world were first suggested by Secretary of State George Marshall in June, 1947. Under the Marshall Plan, as carried out in the following years by the Economic Cooperation Administration, the European nations estimated what they would need to recover and what they could themselves contribute, with the United States supplying the balance of their needs. Many of the items shipped abroad by ECA were industrial implements aiming at restoration of the recipient countries' productive capacity, but vast quantities of grain and other foodstuffs were also supplied. The Marshall Plan was therefore instrumental in averting the possibility of famines, while, at the same time, "it helped to lay the foundation for a sustained period of agricultural prosperity in the United States, thus creating a markedly different situation from that which had caused such early and acute distress in American agriculture after World War I." [31]

The situation was indeed different, and thanks to continued government intervention as well as to the activities of the private trade, agricultural production and exports would expand during the next quarter of a century to unprecedented levels.

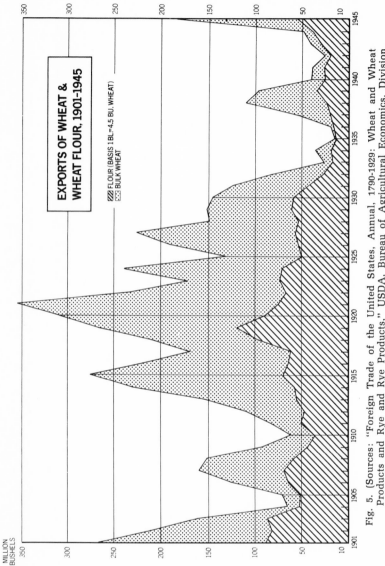

MILLION
BUSHELS

EXPORTS OF WHEAT & WHEAT FLOUR, 1901-1945

▨ FLOUR (BASIS 1 BL=4.5 BU. WHEAT)
⬚ BULK WHEAT

Fig. 5. (Sources: "Foreign Trade of the United States, Annual, 1790-1929: Wheat and Wheat Products and Rye and Rye Products," USDA, Bureau of Agricultural Economics, Division of Statistical and Historical Research, Report FS46, February 8, 1930: "Monthly Summary of Foreign Commerce," (Washington, D. C., Bureau of Foreign and Domestic Commerce, 1901-1945).

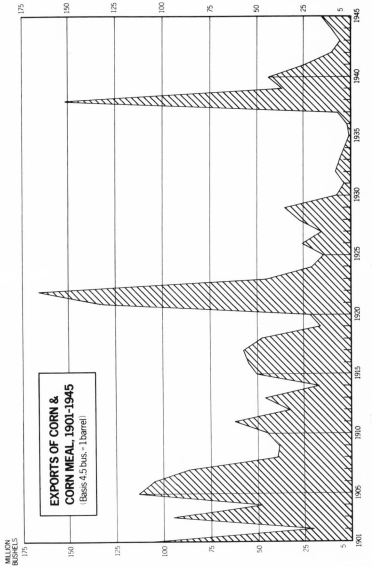

MILLION
BUSHELS

**EXPORTS OF CORN &
CORN MEAL, 1901-1945**
(Basis 4.5 bus. = 1 barrel)

Fig. 6. (Sources: "Foreign Trade of the United States, Annual, 1790-1929: Wheat and Wheat Products and Rye and Rye Products," USDA, Bureau of Agricultural Economics, Division of Statistical and Historical Research, Report FS46, February 8, 1930; "Monthly Summary of Foreign Commerce," (Washington, D. C., Bureau of Foreign and Domestic Commerce, 1901-1945)).

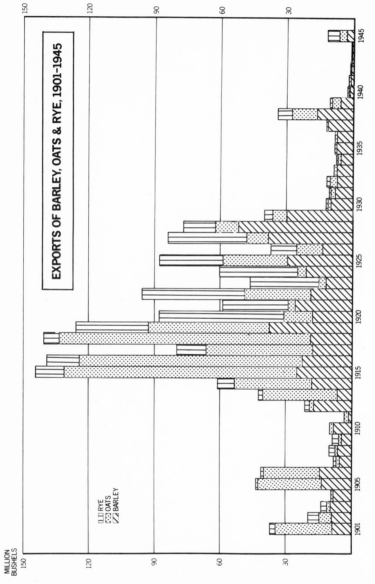

Fig. 7. (Sources: "Foreign Trade of the United States, Annual, 1790-1929: Wheat and Wheat Products and Rye and Rye Products," USDA, Bureau of Agricultural Economics, Division of Statistical and Historical Research, Report FS46, February 8, 1930; "Monthly Summary of Foreign Commerce," (Washington, D. C., Bureau of Foreign and Domestic Commerce, 1901-1945)).

Table 9—Total Exports of Wheat and Flour, 1901-1945
(000 omitted)

Year	Bulk Wheat (bus.)	Wheat Flour (brls.)	Grain Equiv. of Flour (bus.)	Total (bus.)
1901	179,201	19,686	88,587	267,788
1902	129,466	18,327	82,471	211,937
1903	73,373	19,555	87,997	161,370
1904	13,015	11,543	51,943	64,958
1905	20,739	11,314	50,913	71,652
1906	62,851	14,324	64,458	127,309
1907	91,383	15,277	68,746	160,129
1908	92,780	13,013	58,558	151,338
1909	48,481	9,687	43,591	92,072
1910	24,257	8,370	37,665	61,922
1911	32,669	11,258	50,661	83,330
1912	61,655	10,622	47,799	109,454
1913	99,599	12,278	55,251	154,850
1914	173,862	12,769	57,460	231,322
1915	205,926	15,662	70,479	276,405
1916	154,050	14,379	64,705	218,755
1917	106,196	13,926	62,667	168,863
1918	111,177	21,707	97,681	208,858
1919	148,086	26,450	119,025	267,111
1920	218,287	19,854	89,343	309,197
1921	279,949	16,800	75,600	355,549
1922	164,692	15,025	67,612	232,304
1923	98,524	16,310	73,395	171,919
1924	166,302	15,990	71,955	238,257
1925	86,526	11,119	50,035	131,561
1926	138,275	11,850	53,325	191,600
1927	168,307	12,826	57,717	226,024
1928	96,290	11,852	53,334	149,624
1929	90,130	13,663	61,483	151,613
1930	87,774	13,060	58,770	146,544
1931	80,311	9,654	43,443	123,754
1932	54,879	5,796	26,082	80,961
1933	8,883	3,964	17,838	26,721
1934	16,970	4,163	18,733	35,703
1935	233	3,003	13,513	13,746
1936	1,879	3,581	16,114	17,993
1937	34,848	4,363	19,633	54,481
1938	86,902	5,110	22,995	109,897
1939	63,214	7,592	34,164	97,378
1940	14,379	5,658	25,461	39,840
1941	13,109	5,737	25,816	38,925
1942	6,615	4,299	19,345	25,960
1943	11,841	6,623	29,803	41,644
1944	10,029	8,445	38,002	48,031
1945	128,636	12,259	55,165	183,801

93

Table 10—Total Exports of Corn and Corn Meal, 1901-1945
(000 omitted)

Year	Bulk Corn (bus.)	Corn Meal (brls.)	Grain Equiv. of Meal (bus.)	Total (bus.)
1901	102,359	680	3,060	105,419
1902	18,724	256	1,152	19,876
1903	91,733	683	3,073	94,806
1904	46,499	349	1,570	48,069
1905	111,266	481	2,164	113,430
1906	102,519	683	3,073	105,592
1907	83,201	831	3,739	86,940
1908	37,578	359	1,615	39,193
1909	36,205	477	2,146	38,351
1910	42,693	345	1,552	44,245
1911	61,573	300	1,350	62,923
1912	30,980	300	1,350	32,330
1913	45,287	300	1,350	46,637
1914	15,626	348	1,566	17,192
1915	48,264	481	2,164	50,428
1916	53,543	427	1,921	55,464
1917	52,168	1,211	5,449	57,617
1918	39,899	1,790	8,059	47,958
1919	11,193	1,202	5,409	16,602
1920	17,761	867	3,901	21,662
1921	129,055	803	3,613	132,668
1922	163,609	630	2,835	166,444
1923	42,188	624	2,808	44,996
1924	18,366	435	1,957	20,323
1925	12,762	348	1,566	14,328
1926	23,064	516	2,322	25,386
1927	13,428	387	1,741	15,169
1928	25,800	273	1,228	27,028
1929	33,745	267	1,201	34,946
1930	6,369	208	936	7,305
1931	2,700	178	801	3,501
1932	7,856	150	675	8,531
1933	5,364	141	634	5,998
1934	2,987	131	589	3,576
1935	177	101	454	631
1936	524	240	1,080	1,604
1937	5,834	210	945	6,779
1938	147,505	946	4,257	151,762
1939	32,117	952	4,284	36,401
1940	38,317	1,246	5,562	43,879
1941	19,350	1,244	5,598	24,948
1942	9,798	98	441	10,239
1943	5,133	82	369	5,502
1944	10,232	90	405	10,637
1945	15,530	134	603	16,133

Table 11—Total Exports of Barley, Oats and Rye, 1901-1945
(000 omitted)

Year	Barley (bus.)	Oats (bus.)	Rye (bus.)
1901	8,666	25,929	2,618
1902	8,713	5,978	4,855
1903	9,799	1,495	2,758
1904	8,415	1,220	94
1905	13,769	28,822	470
1906	14,528	25,480	1,073
1907	5,444	1,746	1,341
1908	6,671	1,205	2,747
1909	4,589	1,272	368
1910	8,263	1,931	19
1911	1,585	2,044	66
1912	17,536	2,172	1,822
1913	6,645	33,759	2,223
1914	18,208	35,067	7,847
1915	26,529	104,572	13,156
1916	22,486	101,411	15,162
1917	17,859	48,678	13,411
1918	18,805	114,463	7,632
1919	37,612	55,295	32,898
1920	17,854	12,878	57,070
1921	25,834	3,224	29,812
1922	18,781	30,011	47,260
1923	11,983	3,227	30,850
1924	20,712	3,954	35,666
1925	29,089	29,443	28,675
1926	13,586	11,574	11,941
1927	37,973	10,053	35,941
1928	51,677	10,421	14,499
1929	29,523	6,609	3,434
1930	9,874	1,501	266
1931	7,851	2,111	121
1932	7,043	3,486	1,096
1933	7,142	1,476	40
1934	5,447	1,510	121
1935	7,506	508	5
1936	7,377	740	9
1937	11,473	66	248
1938	16,130	11,361	6,578
1939	5,410	4,005	732
1940	1,403	204	245
1941	1,218	530	13
1942	827	416	11
1943	407	121	78
1944	306	292	47
1945	2,809	3,617	4,941

Table 12—Average Grain Prices, 1901-1944
($ per bushel)

Year	Wheat (at Kans. City)	Rye (at Mpls.)	Corn (Farm Value)	Barley (at Chicago)	Oats (at Chicago)
1901	.68	.57	.60	.64	.42
1902	.68	.59	.40	.56	.36
1903	.77	.58	.42	.56	.38
1904	.97	.58	.44	.49	.32
1905	.80	.84	.41	.50	.31
1906	.72	.67	.39	.61	.37
1907	.93	.75	.50	.84	.50
1908	.99	.90	.65	.67	.52
1909	1.07	.82	.62	.67	.42
1910	.98	.77	.52	.92	.34
1911	.97	.95	.68	1.22	.48
1912	.88	.87	.55	.68	.35
1913	.84	.69	.70	.65	.40
1914	1.05	.70	.71	.72	.49
1915	1.19	1.17	.68	.69	.42
1916	1.71	1.06	1.13	1.19	.54
1917	2.52	1.63	1.45	1.46	.71
1918	2.19	1.99	1.52	1.04	.70
1919	2.42	1.95	1.51	1.45	.80
1920	1.83	1.99	.64	.78	.56
1921	1.20	2.03	.52	.61	.35
1922	1.13	1.11	.73	.65	.41
1923	1.05	.92	.81	.72	.44
1924	1.35	.81	1.06	.90	.51
1925	1.63	1.26	.70	.72	.41
1926	1.35	1.07	.74	.77	.43
1927	1.35	1.14	.85	.91	.54
1928	1.12	1.12	.84	.60	.44
1929	1.20	.90	.80	.62	.45
1930	.76	.51	.60	.54	.36
1931	.47	.42	.32	.40	.22
1932	.51	.41	.32	.38	.19
1933	.88	.69	.52	.72	.36
1934	.98	.81	.81	1.05	.48
1935	1.05	.50	.65	.68	.29
1936	1.21	.97	1.04	1.20	.43
1937	1.11	.74	.52	.78	.32
1938	.70	.44	.49	.53	.28
1939	.74	.56	.57	.55	.38
1940	.82	.51	.62	.48	.36
1941	1.12	.65	.75	.65	.49
1942	1.26	.73	.92	.78	.56
1943	1.45	1.08	1.12	1.21	.78
1944	1.56	1.22	1.03	1.19	.74

Notes To Chapter IV

1. Rothstein, *American Wheat,* pp. 278-279.
2. Murray R. Benedict, *Farm Policies of the United States, 1790-1950* (New York: The Twentieth Century Fund, 1953), pp. 112-114.
3. *Ibid.,* p. 140.
4. Emory R. Johnson, T. W. Van Metre, G. G. Huebner, and D. S. Hanchett, *History of Domestic and Foreign Commerce of the United States* (Washington, D.C.: The Carnegie Institution of Washington, 1915), II, p. 89.
5. Tom Gibson Hall, Jr. *Cheap Bread from Dear Wheat: Herbert Hoover, the Wilson Administration, and the Management of Wheat Prices, 1916-1920* (Unpublished Doctoral Dissertation—University of California, Davis, 1968), pp. 48-49.
6. *Ibid.,* p. 7.
7. Frank M. Surface, *The Grain Trade During the World War* (New York: Macmillan Company, 1928), p. 28.
8. *Ibid.,* pp. 62-63.
9. Hall, *Cheap Bread,* p. 113.
10. *Ibid.,* p. 122.
11. *Statistical Abstract of the United States, 1946* (Washington, D.C.: U. S. Department of Commerce, 1947), p. 623.
12. *Ibid.,* p. 573.
13. *Report of the Federal Trade Commission on Methods and Operations of Grain Exporters* (Washington, D. C.: Government Printing Office, 1922-3) II, p. 135.
14. United States Department of Agriculture, *Yearbook 1920,* pp. 496-497.
15. *Report of the Federal Trade Commission,* II, p. 141.
16. United States Department of Agriculture, *Yearbook 1923,* p. 675.
17. Benedict, *Farm Policies,* p. 172.
18. James H. Shideler, *Farm Crisis 1919-1923* (Berkeley and Los Angeles: University of California Press, 1957), p. 123.
19. Benedict, *Farm Policies,* pp. 207-208.
20. George N. Peek, and Hugh S. Johnson, *Equality for Agriculture,* 2nd ed., (Moline, Ill.: Moline Plow Company, 1922), p. 3.
21. *Ibid.,* p. 15
22. *Report of the Federal Trade Commission,* I. XV.
23. Shideler, *Farm Crisis,* p. 284.
24. Benedict, *Farm Policies,* p. 238.
25. Gilbert C. Fite, *George N. Peek and the Fight for Farm Parity* (Norman: University of Oklahoma Press, 1954), p. 78.
26. United States Department of Agriculture, *Yearbook 1933,* p. 415.
27. Van L. Perkins, *Crisis in Agriculture: The Agricultural Adjustment Administration and the New Deal, 1933* (Berkeley and Los Angeles: University of California Press, 1969), p. 11.
28. *Ibid.,* p. 33.
29. *Statistical Abstract of the United States, 1948* (Washington, D.C.: U. S. Department of Commerce, 1949).
30. Benedict, *Farm Policies,* p. 450.
31. *Ibid.,* p. 462.

V

1945-1970: The Staff of Life

The global scope of World War II, and the extent of the destruction and dislocation of agricultural productivity wrought by six years of hostilities in most of Europe and much of Asia, presented the victorious United Nations in the fall and winter of 1945 with a relief task of gigantic proportions. Only the United States, however, having been spared from fighting on home grounds, and having consistently harvested enormous wheat crops during the war years, was in a position to feed the defeated as well as the liberated countries.

As it was, since during the war enormous quantities of wheat were used to make alcohol for synthetic rubber production, the end of hostilities found the United States with a carryover of only about 280 million bushels of wheat,[1] the lowest since 1939, just when export demand appeared from all sides. Fortunately, perfect growing weather and high yields produced a crop of more than one billion bushels, and conversion of grain into alcohol was sharply curtailed, so that in the twelve months beginning July, 1945, almost 400 million bushels of wheat could be exported. By July, 1946, however, the wheat carryover was down to 100 million bushels, and a year later it was further reduced to 83 million, despite harvests of 1.1 and 1.3 billion bushels in 1946 and 1947 respectively. The greatly expanded production was, of course, the result of accelerated wartime technological change, as well as favorable weather conditions, though the caprice of weather was minimized by the new technology. But it seemed, at war's end, that even the larger crops would be barely adequate. A main cause of this disappearance of stockpiles was the pressing need of overseas populations, especially in Europe where a very severe winter in 1946 had been followed by extensive drought in 1947. American wheat exports in these two crucial years amounted to 397 million bushels in 1946 and 495 million in 1947. Indicative of the plight of the recipient countries, whose milling industry had been

99

devastated, was the fact that close to one-half of the wheat was exported at this time in the form of flour, ready for distribution and consumption.

The pressing needs of Asian countries in the immediate postwar period also brought about a sharp increase in overseas shipment of another food grain; rice. Exports, which in the 1930s had never exceeded a yearly average of 5 million bags of 100 pounds, spurted to more than 10 million bags in 1945, 11.5 million bags in 1946, and 12.2 million in 1947.

Distribution in Germany and Japan was handled by the allied military governments, while in other countries such as Poland, Yugoslavia, Greece, Italy, Czechoslovakia and China the task fell to the United Nations Relief and Rehabilitation Administration, commonly referred to as UNRRA, under the direction of former New York Governor Herbert Lehman.

Grain shipments, incidentally, were greatly helped by the abundant availability of freight space, no longer needed to transport war materials and troops. Hundreds of the 10,000-ton Liberty ships launched during the war were pressed into this service, which they continued to fulfill for many years until they were gradually replaced by larger and more modern ships, primarily bulk carriers whose unobstructed holds could be more easily and speedily filled and unloaded. On occasion, tankers were also used to carry grain instead of petroleum or other liquids.

By 1948, the establishment of the European Economic Cooperation Administration to implement the Marshall Plan was giving unprecedented impetus to grain exports, of which wheat and flour represented by far the major proportion. Exports of bulk wheat in 1948 were 375 million bushels, while another 129 million bushels were exported as flour; the resulting total of 504 million bushels would not be exceeded until 1956.

In addition, significant shifts in the United States agricultural export trade became evident in 1948. One of the most significant changes was the reduced importance of the United Kingdom as a market. While Great Britain had taken 35 percent of total American agricultural exports in 1938, it accounted for a mere 6 percent in 1948. The greatest decrease in American trade with England was in grain exports, which from a value of $50 million in 1938 virtually disappeared ten years later. On the other hand, the continental countries of Western Europe, which in 1938 had taken 29 percent of United States agricultural exports, raised their share to 55 percent in 1948, primarily as a result of heavy wheat shipments under the various United States assistance programs. Altogether, 75 percent of total wheat exports in 1948 were financed by U. S. government programs, while much of the remaining 25 percent was exported to countries in Central and Latin America which had accumulated dollars as a result of large wartime purchases by the United States in those areas.[2]

Another factor making the year 1948 stand out was the passage of the first comprehensive agricultural legislation since the war. To stimulate production, Congress had guaranteed in 1942 that farm prices would be supported at 90 percent of parity for two years after the end of hostilities. President Harry Truman had declared the war ended on December 31, 1946 with the result that wartime guarantees would be automatically terminated at the end of 1948.

The election of 1946 had given the Republicans control of Congress for the first time since 1930, but the division between congressional representatives from the farm states ran more along geographic than party lines. Most of the southeastern congressmen and senators advocated high and rigid price supports, while many representatives of the Middle West and the Northeast favored a return to a free economy. Accordingly, after extensive hearings in 1947, in March, 1948, Sen. George Aiken of Vermont introduced a bill establishing supports at flexible levels depending on the size of harvests, while Representative Clifford Hope of Kansas pushed through the House a bill extending mandatory supports at 90 percent of parity. After a bitter and protracted fight, Congress approved in June the Agricultural Act of 1948, which was in reality a juxtaposition of the two bills. A particularly significant element of the new bill was a revised formula for determining parity levels, which clearly aimed at discouraging overproduction, especially for those commodities which could be produced more cheaply than in the 1909-1914 base period. Before the effects of the new act could be felt, however, a landslide vote reelected Harry Truman to the presidency and returned control of both Houses of Congress to the Democrats. The chairmanship of the House Committee on Agriculture, therefore, passed to Harold Cooley of North Carolina, and that of the Senate Committee on Agriculture and Forestry to Elmer Thomas of Oklahoma. Both Representative Cooley and Senator Thomas were advocates of high mandatory supports for farm products, and their views prevailed the following year over those of both the Republican group, led by Hope and Aiken, and the advocates of the administration-backed Brannan Plan. This plan, submitted to Congress in April, 1949, by Secretary of Agriculture Charles F. Brannan, represented a new departure in government assistance to agriculture, in that it foresaw the computation of price support levels on the basis of income standards, and it also limited the size of farm operation that would be eligible to receive support payments for its whole production. Violently opposed by all farm organizations except the Farmers Union, and tepidly received by Congress, the Brannan Plan was the object of considerable controversy and finally came to nothing.[3] Instead, in October, 1949, Congress passed the Agricultural Act of 1949, which effectively blocked the downward readjustment of the parity formula and established high mandatory support levels for most farm commodities, with the result of continued high production levels.

Nineteen-forty-nine also saw the conclusion of the first International Wheat Agreement, a significant step toward normalization and regulation of the world wheat trade. Abortive attempts in this direction had been made as early as 1933, and several International Wheat Conferences had been held during the war and in the years immediately after.

Finally, early in 1949, an agreement was reached in Washington between four exporting countries (United States, Canada, Australia and France), and thirty-seven importing countries, whereby each country was assigned a wheat quota, and minimum and maximum prices of $1.50 and $1.80 a bushel were set. Each importing country assumed the obligation to buy its quota if it were offered at the minimum price, and each exporting country undertook to sell its quota if it were bid the maximum price.

An increasing share of world trade in wheat and flour was by now again being handled by the private trade in both exporting and importing countries. As world wheat prices, although lower than the $2.80 a bushel reached in the immediate postwar period, were still appreciably higher than the agreement maximum, most importers were glad to buy their guaranteed quota under the agreement, and during its first year of operation sales under the IWA accounted for more than half of total world trade. By now, however, European agriculture was recovering, and the need for emergency supplies of wheat and flour to relieve food shortages was becoming less acute. As a result, even though wheat acreage in 1949 reached the all-time record of 84 million acres, and production exceeded 1 billion bushels, total United States exports of wheat and flour in the 1949 crop year were down to 300 million bushels, of which about 160 million bushels moved under the International Wheat Agreement. To compensate exporters for the difference between the domestic price of wheat and the IWA price, the Commodity Credit Corporation paid them a subsidy which averaged 54 cents a bushel.

The overexpanded wheat acreage, coupled with declining exports and the maintenance of the price support at 90 percent of parity, or $1.95 a bushel, caused a sharp increase in the quantity of wheat put under loan. By July, 1950, the Commodity Credit Corporation owned 361 million bushels of wheat.

The outbreak of the Korean War caused an upsurge of scare buying which continued through 1951. Prices rose to more than $2.00 a bushel, thus exceeding support levels and reducing appreciably the quantities put under CCC loan. Total wheat and flour exports rose to 366 million bushels in 1950 and to 475 million the following year, of which more than half moved under the terms of the International Wheat Agreement.

The year 1952 marked the beginning of a steady and burdensome increase in CCC wheat stocks. Production, thanks to continued large acreage and exceptionally high yields, exceeded 1.3 billion bushels, while exports dropped sharply to 317 million bushels. By the end of the 1952-53 crop year, almost 500 million bushels of wheat were owned or controlled by CCC.

Another bumper crop in 1953 produced 1.1 billion bushels of wheat. The International Wheat Agreement had been renewed in 1953 for an additional three years, but nevertheless exports were down to a mere 216 million bushels, while support levels, owing to the general price rise following the Korean crisis, averaged $2.21 a bushel, causing about half the crop to be put under loan. By the end of June, 1954, the wheat carryover in the United States had reached 903 million bushels, of which 850 million were held by the government.

Since CCC had no storage facilities of its own, large quantities of grain were loaded on the vast "mothball fleet" of Liberty and Victory ships anchored in the Hudson River, but the mounting flood of grain surpluses also gave tremendous impetus to the construction of warehouses and elevators by merchants and exporters, who in turn leased all or most of the storage space to the government. It was obvious that a cost and storage problem of unmanageable proportions was in the making, and that steps must be taken to reduce wheat production or increase wheat disposal, or, hopefully, both. To the first end, in accordance with the provisions of the Agricultural Act of 1938, as amended in 1948 and 1949, and with the concurrence of a farmers' referendum, the acreage to be seeded in wheat for the 1954 crop year was restricted to 62 million acres, rather than the 78 millon average of the previous three years. Also, translating into law the laissez-faire philosophy of Ezra Taft Benson, the first Republican secretary of agriculture in twenty years, the Agricultural Act of 1954 provided that in future years support could be gradually reduced to as low as 75 percent of parity. The 1954 crop, however, thanks to increased use of fertilizer and high yields, was still close to the billion bushel level. To promote exports, it was clearly necessary to embark on aggressive and heavily subsidized disposal activities. Thus the PL 480 program was born.

The Agricultural Trade Development and Assistance Act of 1954, commonly referred to as Public Law 480, had its origins in hearings called by the Senate Committee on Agriculture and Forestry in July, 1953, to consider legislation giving President Dwight Eisenhower emergency authority to use farm surpluses for famine relief in foreign countries. Testifying before the committee, Sen. Hubert Humphrey of Minnesota outlined a vastly expanded program of surplus disposal, going far beyond the proposed legislation.

Among the proposals advocated by Senator Humphrey were the main features of what, a year later and after considerable debate in both houses of Congress, would be enacted as Public Law 480: sale of surplus agricultural commodities to foreign countries for payment in local currencies of restricted use, donation of food supplies to disaster areas and to welfare organizations, barter of surplus farm products for goods required by the national stockpiles of the United States.

In its first year of operation, the provisions of PL 480 helped raise American wheat and flour exports to 274 million bushels, of which 158 were financed by government programs. During the following two years, the rise in volume and proportional financing was dramatically on the increase, for in the year beginning July 1, 1955, the United States exported 240 million bushels of wheat under government programs and 105 million for dollars, while during the next twelve months the figures were 375 and 174 million bushels respectively. The 1956 total exports of 549 million bushels of wheat would not be surpassed until the expansion of the Food for Peace program by the Kennedy administration in 1961. While the major portion of the wheat exports financed by PL 480 moved under the provisions of Title I, in exchange for foreign currencies, sizable quantities of CCC-held grain were also bartered on an equivalent value basis for foreign-produced goods, mostly strategic raw materials, to be added to the national stockpile. Such barters had actually begun with specific congressional authority in 1948 and 1949, but the provisions of Title III of PL 480, constituting an actual legislative mandate to expand barter activities, gave impetus to the program and resulted in increased overseas shipments of agricultural commodities, of which wheat represented the largest percentage.

Besides the various disposal techniques instituted under PL 480, wheat exports in the 1950s were also expanded by shipments under the Mutual Security Acts and the Act for International Development (AID), which sent overseas quantities of wheat ranging from 70 million bushels in 1954 to 13 million bushels in 1959, and which were phased out during the following decade.

Thus, as the decade of the 1950s drew to a close, there was no lack of efforts and programs trying to promote the export of American wheat, but the results of these attempts at reducing surpluses were largely frustrated by the combination of continued high domestic production and reduced foreign demand. The U. S. wheat carryover on July 1, 1960, reached 1.3 billion bushels, or just about the same as that year's bumper crop. Spurred by government programs as well as by the proselytizing work of the U.S.D.A.'s Foreign Agricultural Service in cooperation with American Farm Trade Associations, 1960-61 exports rose to a record 661 million bushels, but this was not sufficient to prevent a further increase in the carryover to 1.4 billion bushels. The next year, exports rose further, to 719 million bushels, while acreage reduction in 1962 cut production back to 1.1 billion bushels. Then came the famous summer of 1963, when the wheat harvests of Russia and Eastern Europe were 20 percent below normal, and the Soviet bloc appeared as a new market for vast quantities of wheat, of which more than 100 million bushels came from the United States. Shortly thereafter, a severe drought hit India, and PL 480 shipments of wheat to that country rose to unprecedented heights, 244 million bushels in 1965-66 and 171 million the following year. Pakistan and Brazil also received very sizable quantities under PL 480. As a result of these developments, American wheat exports which already in 1963-64 had reached 856 million bushels, rose in 1965-66 to the all-time high of 867 million. By July 1, 1966, the wheat carryover in the United States had declined to 425 million bushels, the lowest since 1952. However, under the influence of the neo-Malthusian theories which gained widespread circulation in the mid-sixties, pointing out that the earth's population was increasing much faster than food supplies, in the summer of 1966 wheat acreage allotments in the United States were increased by one-third to 68 million acres, and as a result more than 1.5 billion bushels of wheat were harvested in 1967.

That the fears of world starvation prevalent at the time were not justified was clearly shown by the developments of the following years, which included not only a sharp rise in production and stocks in the traditional exporting countries, but also vital changes in the domestic agriculture and trading patterns of traditional importers.

Many PL 480 agreements contained a stipulation, insisted upon by the United States government, that part of the local currencies obtained by recipient countries from the sale of the American commodities be used for the improvement of their own agriculture with the ultimate goal of self-sufficiency. The Ford Foundation, the Rockefeller Foundation, and other American philanthropic organizations were also instrumental in financing research. As a result, a new short-stemmed, high-yielding, disease-resistant variety of wheat was developed in Mexico in the 1950s by the American plant pathologist Norman Borlaug, who in 1970 was awarded the Nobel Peace Prize for this achievement. During the same period the International Rice Research Institute at Los-Banos, in the Philippines, developed the new "miracle rice," IR-8, which also produced dramatically higher yields. The improvement in these two grains, which are the backbone of the world's food supply, has rightly been called the Green Revolution. Thanks to this new technology, production of food grains in the developing countries increased dramatically, especially on the Indian subcontinent, where at the end of the decade the combination of increased wheat production and the beginning of efforts towards population control gave rise to the expectation of self-sufficiency.

Furthermore, unlikely as it may have seemed at the time these programs were launched by humanitarian as well as political motivations, the success of these programs raised the possibility that some of these countries might soon be able to increase their grain production to such an extent as to become substantial competitors in shrinking world markets.

Europe, of course, had after the war enjoyed the same technological improvements as the United States, and had been generally able to increase grain production very substantially, both in total volume and on a yield-per-acre basis. At the same time, burgeoning economic protectionism in Western Europe drastically altered agricultural production and deeply affected American wheat exports there. The goal of economic union set by the signing of the Treaty of Rome in March, 1957, by Belgium, France, the Netherlands, Luxembourg, West Germany, and Italy, included the establishment of a Common Agricultural Policy, the implementation of which from 1962 on resulted in a tremendous expansion of wheat production, especially in France.

By the end of the 1960s the Common Market, as the European Economic Community is generally called, was subsidizing production of wheat and other farm products by guaranteeing farmers and grain merchants "intervention prices," which were far above world prices. To prevent imports from depressing Common Market prices, variable levies were imposed which in some cases almost doubled the price at which foreign grain was sold at Rotterdam, and effectively limited imports to those varieties such as durum for spaghetti manufacturing and high-protein hard bread types of which European production was still limited. Since there were no production controls, a heavy wheat glut developed, and the Common Market emerged as an aggressive wheat exporter, granting export subsidies well in excess of $1.00 a bushel. Furthermore, subsidies were given for the denaturing of wheat by the admixture of fish oil, rendering the grain unpalatable for human consumption but making it more than competitive for cattle feeding and, in turn, reducing the volume of feed grain imports. Intra-Common Market wheat trade naturally boomed, more than quadrupling in the decade of the 1960s, with France originating 90 percent of this trade.

United States wheat exports naturally suffered from these developments and declined appreciably towards the end of the decade, despite promotional efforts by the U. S. government and by the private trade. The only bright spot was provided by Japan, where market development work by the U.S.D.A. and by Western Wheat Associates, USA, Inc., resulted in a 40 percent increase in flour production and use from 1960 through 1969, and a rise in per capita consumption during the same period from fifty-seven pounds a year to more than seventy.[4] As a result, Japan in 1970 became the first country to purchase for dollars in a given year more than 100 million bushels of American wheat, and the first country to import over a billion dollars of U. S. agricultural products in one year.[5] It should not be forgotten, of course, that it was the United States' liberal import policy which made it possible for Japan to earn the foreign exchange to pay for these agricultural imports.

There were also, in the decade of the sixties, a number of attempts towards international management of grain surpluses. These attempts included the various negotiations at Geneva under the General Agreement on Tariffs and Trade which culminated in the inconclusive "Kennedy Round," as well as the replacement in 1967 of the oft-renewed and expanded but largely ineffective International Wheat Agreement with an International Grain Arrangement, which, in turn, proved unworkable and gave way in 1971 to a new and mainly uncommercial International Wheat Agreement.

More imaginative and practical techniques employed by the U. S. government to promote agricultural exports ranged from the Payment-in-kind Program, which used wheat from government stocks to pay export subsidies due to commercial shippers, to the CCC Export Credit Sales Program, which underwrote financing of commercial sales for up to three years at attractive interest rates. And finally, in 1970, wheat acreage allotment was reduced to 45.5 million acres, the lowest since the restrictions had started in 1938, and fifty percent below the 1966-67 peak, while passage by Congress of the Agricultural Act of 1970 endeavored to establish for the United States a "market-oriented" farm policy. Referred to as the "set-aside" bill, the act was said to aim at "giving farmers maximum freedom to pursue lower cost of production and maximum sales . . . both at home and abroad," [6] by being allowed, after setting aside the allotted share of the national land diversion requirements, to plant on the remaining acres the crop or crops giving the greatest net return. With wheat support price set at only $1.25 a bushel, the act obviously represented an effort to reduce wheat production and shift farm productivity to other crops such as oilseeds and feed grains, for which greater world demand existed. Whether this goal could be achieved must be assessed by future historians.

No study of American cereal exports in the postwar period would be complete without mention of the two principal food grains besides wheat: rye and rice.

Rye, which was once the most common bread grain in Northern and Central Europe, and an important staple in this country, gradually diminished in volume until it represented but a small fraction of world shipments. The reason for the decline can be found in changes in food preference in some countries, but it must be traced primarily to growing affluence in the Western World causing wheat to replace rye as the staple bread grain of the masses. American exports of rye, which in 1922 had reached a peak of 101 million bushels, only to fall to virtually nothing by 1930, in the decades after World War II accounted for only a few million bushels each year. The only exceptions were 1956 and 1963, when 10 million bushels were exported, and 1962 which saw exports of about 20 million bushels, due to a large crop on expanded acreage resulting from a sharp reduction in wheat allotments.

As to rice, which is, after all, the principal food for more than one-third of the world's population, the war and early postwar years saw the United States boost its production to unparalleled levels, so that exports in the mid-1940s were more than double the average of the preceding decade. As is generally the case, however, the crop expansion encouraged by foreign needs went too far. By 1956, as Asian rice-exporting countries were regaining their prewar market position, the United States, despite continuing high exports, mostly with PL 480 financing, found itself with a rough rice carryover of almost 35 million hundredweights, or 70 percent of that year's total crop. The alternative was between a sharp curtailment of production and an all-out market development effort, and the second route was chosen. The rice industry's promotional arm, the U. S. Rice Export Development Association, jointly with the U.S.D.A.'s Foreign Agricultural Service, embarked on a world-wide campaign aimed at creating consumer demand for American long-grain rice, the success of which could be gauged by the fact that whereas in the late 1950s only about thirty-five countries were buying American rice for dollars, by the end of the following decade the number of such foreign markets had risen to 110. This market expansion in the 1960s permitted the United States to maintain a steadily rising volume of both production and exports, despite the loss of the Cuban market which used to take more than 4 million bags a year, and the disappearance of other markets such as the Philippines, where the development of the high-yielding "miracle rice" brought about complete self-sufficiency. Whereas total exports of American milled rice in 1954 had fallen to 9 million bags, in 1967 they reached a peak of 41 million bags, and accounted for only slightly smaller yearly volumes during the rest of the decade. Furthermore, shipments for dollars, except in 1962 and in 1968, consistently and substantially exceeded those made for payment in foreign currencies under PL 480. As a result, during the 1960s, the United States surpassed Burma, China, and Thailand, and climbed from fourth to first place among the world's top rice exporters.

One of the Four Freedoms enunciated by President Franklin Roosevelt in 1941 was Freedom from Want. Undoubtedly the most vital facet of this basic right is freedom from hunger, because, as Arnold Toynbee pointed out to the first F.A.O. World Food Congress twenty-two years later, "a human being who is short of food will find that all other forms of wealth are valueless to him." "Since our ancestors first became human," Toynbee also stated, "most human beings have been hungry for most of the time. . . . Happily . . . there must be a huge unrealized potential of human energy and creativity which could be released for the service of human welfare if the hunger that has been coeval with humanity were to be abolished by a definitive victory in our Freedom from Hunger Campaign." [7] From the very beginning of colonization, but more particularly in recent times, American exports of food grains have been strongly contributing to the realization of that goal.

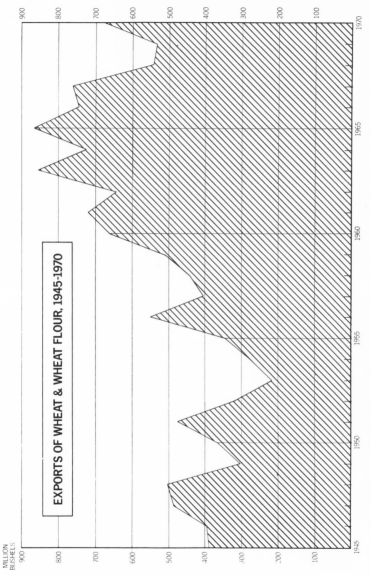

MILLION
BUSHELS

EXPORTS OF WHEAT & WHEAT FLOUR, 1945-1970

Fig. 8. (Source: United States Department of Agriculture, **Agricultural Statistics** (Washington, D. C.: United States Printing Office, 1967, 1970, 1971)).

TABLE 13—WHEAT STATISTICS,

Year Beginning July 1	ACREAGE		Yield Per Harvested Acre (bus. per a.)	Production (mill. bus.)	Domestic Use (Seed, Food, Feed etc.) (mill. bus.)
	Seeded (mill. a.)	Harvested (mill. a.)			
1945	69.1	65.2	17.0	1.108	899.1
1946	71.6	67.1	17.2	1,152	771.8
1947	78.3	74.5	18.2	1,359	761.7
1948	78.3	72.4	17.9	1,295	681.4
1949	83.9	75.9	14.5	1,098	680.3
1950	71.3	61.6	16.5	1,019	689.8
1951	78.5	61.9	16.0	988	688.6
1952	78.6	71.1	18.4	1,306	661.0
1953	78.9	67.8	17.3	1,173	633.9
1954	62.5	54.4	18.1	984	611.4
1955	58.2	47.3	19.8	937	603.7
1956	60.7	49.8	20.2	1,005	588.7
1957	49.8	43.8	21.8	956	591.6
1958	56.0	53.0	27.5	1,457	608.6
1959	56.7	51.7	21.6	1,118	596.9
1960	54.9	51.9	26.1	1,355	603.4
1961	55.7	51.6	23.9	1,232	608.0
1962	49.3	43.7	25.0	1,092	580.4
1963	53.4	45.5	25.2	1,147	588.4
1964	55.7	49.8	25.8	1,283	643.6
1965	57.4	49.6	26.5	1,316	731.2
1966	54.4	49.9	26.3	1,312	679.3
1967	67.8	58.8	25.9	1,522	647.8
1968	62.5	55.3	28.5	1,576	754.0
1969	54.3	47.6	30.7	1,459	791.0
1970	49.6	44.3	31.1	1,378	780.0

1945-1970

WHEAT & FLOUR EXPORTS				SEASON'S AVERAGE PRICES			
Under Gov't. Program (mill. bus.)	For Dollars (mill. bus.)	Total (mill. bus.)	Exports as Percentage of Production	Rec'd. by Farmers ($ per bus.)	At Kansas City ($ per bus.)	EXPORTS	
						Wheat ($ per bus.)	Flour ($ per CWT)
NA	NA	389.6	35.2	1.49	1.60	1.58	3.08
NA	NA	396.7	34.4	1.90	2.09	2.06	5.77
NA	NA	485.2	35.7	2.29	2.52	2.82	6.76
376.0	127.6	503.6	38.9	1.98	2.19	2.58	6.21
256.0	46.1	302.9	27.6	1.88	2.16	2.31	5.66
173.0	192.9	365.9	35.9	2.00	2.28	2.01	5.45
159.3	315.7	475.0	48.1	2.11	2.43	2.26	5.34
29.6	287.9	317.5	24.3	2.09	2.32	2.13	5.56
100.5	116.2	216.7	18.5	2.04	2.27	2.05	5.23
158.0	116.0	274.0	27.8	2.12	2.37	1.78	4.38
240.7	105.3	346.0	36.9	1.98	2.18	1.70	4.24
375.1	174.0	549.1	54.6	1.97	2.21	1.73	4.37
246.7	155.6	402.3	42.1	1.93	2.15	1.76	4.61
303.0	139.8	442.8	30.4	1.75	1.94	1.72	4.33
374.6	135.2	509.8	45.6	1.76	2.00	1.69	4.12
457.7	203.8	661.5	48.8	1.74	1.94	1.72	4.23
491.1	228.3	719.4	58.4	1.83	2.05	1.80	3.99
485.4	158.4	643.8	59.0	2.04	2.25	1.82	4.14
503.4	352.7	856.1	74.6	1.85	1.94	1.79	4.01
567.3	157.7	725.0	56.5	1.37	1.57	1.73	4.07
568.0	298.4	867.4	65.9	1.35	1.61	1.62	3.99
372.8	371.5	744.3	56.7	1.63	1.85	1.77	4.38
471.2	289.9	761.1	50.0	1.39	1.59	1.70	3.78
299.1	245.0	544.1	34.5	1.24	1.46	1.67	3.98
308.8	225.9	534.7	36.6	1.23	1.45	1.57	3.87
368.5	307.8	676.3	49.0	1.36	1.54	1.65	3.90

BREAD UPON THE WATERS

Notes To Chapter V

1. This and all subsequent statistical data in the chapter are drawn from: United States Department of Agriculture, *Agricultural Statistics* (Washington, D.C.: United States Printing Office, 1967, 1970, 1971).

2. G. N. Chumley, "Postwar Shifts in U. S. Agricultural Export Trade," *Foreign Agriculture,* Vol. XIII, No. 11 (November, 1949), pp. 256-258.

3. Reo M. Christenson, *The Brannan Plan—Farm Politics and Policy* (Ann Arbor: University of Michigan Press, 1959), *passim.*

4. Richard E. Bell, "U. S. Wheat Sales to Japan—a Payoff for U. S. Market Development," *Foreign Agriculture,* Vol. IX, No. 16 (April 19, 1971), p. 3.

5. Dewain H. Rahe and Isaac E. Lemon, "The First Billion Dollar Customer," *Foreign Agriculture,* Vol. VIII, No. 35 (August 31, 1970), pp. 2-5.

6. Carroll G. Brunthaver, "Agricultural Act of 1970—Its Trade Implications," *Foreign Agriculture,* Vol. VIII, No. 49 (December 7, 1970), pp. 2-3.

7. "Arnold J. Toynbee Speaks on Man and Hunger," *Foreign Agriculture,* Vol. I (June 17, 1963), pp. 4-5.

VI

1945-1970: Feed Grains, Unlimited

The end of World War II found the United States with a heavy pent-up domestic demand for meat products, and thus a ready outlet for its vastly expanded production of feed grains, while the depletion of animal stocks in the war ravaged countries of Europe and Asia caused a sharp decline in their need for feedstuffs. Expansion of United States feed grain exports, therefore, was by no means as rapid as that experienced by food grains.

In any event, exports of coarse grains, as corn, grain sorghum, barley and oats are collectively called, never historically accounted for more than a small percentage of United States production, since most of these grains are either fed by the growers directly to their own livestock or sold to other farmers for the same purpose. In the 1890s, for instance, American exports of corn reached levels which would not be surpassed for six decades, but even at their highest, in 1898, they represented only 9.3 percent of the total crop.[1] When considered in relation to the magnitude of American harvests, however, even relatively low percentages loom large in sheer volume, making feed grains one of the most important components in United States farm exports. Their history is therefore a proper subject for examination, especially in view of the high and expanding exports of some items in recent times.

The very first postwar year saw exports of only 31 million bushels of corn, 9 of barley, and 1 of sorghum.[2] Oats exports, at 21 million bushels, were larger than at any time since 1925, but whereas the other feed grains were destined, in the subsequent decades, to regain and amply exceed the higher export levels reached in earlier periods, oats exports remained within their basic historical range, never again even approaching the highs briefly touched during World War I. This was due, not only to a steady fall in production, reflecting reduced demand caused by the decline in numbers of draft animals, but also to the fact that

115

oats, because of their bulkiness, cost more than other grains to transport on a per ton basis.

Barley exports, on the other hand, showed a steady if slow increase from the end of World War II until 1960, but then they began declining just as steadily to almost negligible proportions.

The two feed grains which grabbed the spotlight during the last quarter of a century were corn and sorghum. There is, after all, good reason why these two are for export the most popular of the four main feed grains. Because of their higher specific weights, they are far more economical to ship than barley and oats, while their feeding value is also proportionally higher. It is therefore the history of their exports, especially corn, which deserves a more detailed analysis.

With the end of price controls in 1946, the corn market advanced rapidly and American farmers, thanks to the use of improved hybrid varieties and favorable weather, obtained a record yield and harvested a record crop. Then the catastrophic weather of 1946-47 in Europe caused a spurt of demand for all grains, so that exports of American corn jumped to 136 million bushels, the largest volume since 1937, and those of sorghum to 24 million bushels. The next year, however, severe droughts in the United States caused a sharp decline in yields as well as in harvested acreage, and corn exports slumped to a mere 15 million bushels, less than even sorghum at 17 million, while the short crop reduced the carryover stocks to the lowest level since 1936. Prices naturally skyrocketed, reaching the all-time high of $2.40 a bushel in September, 1947.

The next year, even though the acreage was no larger, the unprecedented yield of 43 bushels per acre produced a corn crop which for the first time in history exceeded 3 billion bushels. This huge harvest, accompanied as it was by an appreciable reduction in the number of hogs on farms, produced a supply which was fully adequate to restore the carryover to its normal level. The supply was also sufficient to meet current needs, including exports, which rose again to 118 million bushels and remained at approximately that level for the next two years.

Meanwhile, Congress passed the Agricultural Act of 1948, which would have instituted a new method of computing support parities, but was almost immediately superseded by the Act of 1949 which, in effect, reaffirmed and raised average parity levels. With prices declining to less than the guaranteed 90 percent of parity, more and more farmers chose to put corn under government loan, and by October, 1950, CCC holdings reached a new high of 650 million bushels.

The inflationary upsurge in prices which followed the outbreak of war in Korea in the summer of 1950 caused an increase in domestic and foreign demand sufficient to permit some reduction in CCC corn stocks, and they shrank to 300 million bushels by the end of the 1951 season. Also, thanks to a favorable price relationship with other grains, sorghum exports increased to 75 million bushels in 1950-51 and held at 62 million the following year, while corn exports fell to 82 million bushels. In 1952-53, due to comparative pricing, the situation was reversed, and corn exports rose to 145 million bushels while barely 10 million bushels of sorghum were exported.

Despite some reductions in acreage, large crops in 1952 and 1953 brought renewed increases in government stocks; once again vast quantities of corn were put under loan, and CCC holdings and commitments climbed to an all-time high of 760 million bushels by the end of the 1953 season.

In an attempt to contain the increasing size of CCC-held surpluses, the government tried to restrain corn production in 1954 by means of acreage allotments, but the reduction was more than made up by an expansion in the acreage planted to sorghum, barley, and oats. Sorghum production doubled, and even though 48 million bushels of this grain were exported along with 104 million bushels of corn, it was obvious that more drastic steps were needed to bring production and use into better balance. In April, 1954, the Department of Agriculture offered to sell 170 million bushels of 1948 and 1949 corn at reduced prices reflecting off-grade condition, and the following month it announced a program whereby feed grains from CCC stocks would be made available for export at prices lower than those prevailing in the domestic market. The subsidies offered by this program, however, being limited to 15 cents a bushel for corn and barley, and 10 cents a bushel for oats, had only a very limited effect in increasing exports, while the quantities being added to government stocks continued to mount. In 1954, 114 million bushels each of barley and sorghum were put under CCC loan, representing 31 percent and 56 percent respectively of the year's crops.[3]

Here too, as in wheat exports, the situation was rescued by the passage and implementation of PL 480. Out of total feed grain

117

exports of 318 million bushels in 1955, 183 million moved under government programs, primarily barters, and a similar situation prevailed in 1956 when exactly half of the 295 million bushels of feed grains exported was covered by donations, barters, and sales for foreign currency under PL 480.

After the first beneficial impact of government programs, however, feed grain exports began a decade of meteoric expansion under the spur of purely economic stimuli. The world's principal importers of feed grains, after all, have always been the developed countries, particularly Western Europe and Japan. By 1957, postwar recovery and the resulting rising incomes in these countries were boosting demand for meat, poultry, and dairy products, and consequently triggering accelerated growth in their livestock industries. To indicate the potential usage of feed grains, suffice it to say that while yearly per capita consumption of red meat in the United States in 1958 was 160 pounds, the comparable figure for the six Common Market countries was only eighty-six pounds, with Italy at the bottom of the scale with forty pounds per person. Poultry consumption in 1958 was almost thirty-two pounds per person in the United States, and a mere seven pounds a head in the Common Market. In Europe and Japan the time was therefore ripe for large-scale adoption of the management and feeding techniques that had earlier revolutionized the livestock industry in the United States. And the United States, as the world's largest and most efficient producer of feed grains, stood ready to fill any increase in world demand. While production increased, coming close to the 4 billion bushel level in both 1959 and 1960, corn exports climbed to 230 million bushels each in 1958 and 1959, 292 million in 1960, and 435 million in 1961. Sorghum exports also reached new highs, with shipments in those four years of 100, 98, 71, and 99 million bushels. Even barley touched its peak volumes in this period, with 117 million bushels exported in 1958, 118 million in 1959, and 86 and 84 million the next two years.

Helping the expansion of feed grain exports in this period as well as during the following years was also the opening in 1959 of the St. Lawrence Seaway, bringing to a successful completion a development program which had begun more than two centuries earlier. Until 1779, the treacherous Lachine Rapids had forced ships sailing up the St. Lawrence to stop at Montreal. That year, the British built five stone locks around the rapids, allowing passage of the flat-bottomed boats then in use. As time passed, more locks and canals were built, a connection was established between Lake Ontario and Lake Erie to by-pass Niagara Falls, and a series of locks was built at Sault Ste. Marie to open up Lake Superior. By 1908 ships could travel from the Atlantic Ocean to the Great Lakes, but the maximum draft of fourteen feet greatly limited the size of vessels which could complete the journey. In 1954, 419 years after Jacques Cartier had discovered and named the St. Lawrence, a joint U. S.-Canadian effort began construction of a twenty-seven-foot channel, which, at a cost of $471 million, was completed in June, 1959. The results were immediate and spectacular. Besides a burgeoning two-way traffic of other raw materials and manufactured products, in 1960 there were 18 million bushels of American wheat and 48 million bushels of corn shipped through the Seaway, much of this tonnage being loaded directly on ocean-going vessels at such inland ports as Duluth, Chicago, and Toledo. By 1968, those quantities would be more than tripled, while further harbor improvements and elevator construction would insure the continued growth of this avenue for American grain exports.

Turning once more to a review of American feed grain exports, we find that 1963, a banner year for wheat, established new records also for corn and sorghum, with exports of 500 and 117 million bushels respectively. The main reason for this further increase was the poor harvest in Eastern Europe, normally a supplier to some Western European countries. For a time there were even indications that the Soviet Union might buy U. S. corn as well as wheat, but Russian purchases did not materialize. In 1963, American feed grain exports were the highest ever to the Netherlands, Italy, and Spain, the latter country being particularly noteworthy for having evolved from a feed grain importer under PL 480 to a large dollar market. Another all-time trade record was established with Japan, which also experienced a poor grain crop in 1963, and was forced to revise her feed grain import requirements upwards, the largest portion of which came from the United States.

The following year, 1964-65, saw another record breaking performance by American feed grain exporters. The West German potato crop was much reduced, and pasture and hay production was below normal, while hog numbers were at record levels. Most of the rest of Europe did experience good harvests, but the Spanish grain crop was extremely poor, and Spain's import needs,

119

because of the dramatic growth in feed manufacturing and livestock feeding, were sharply higher. In Japan, a continuing dietary shift from fish to livestock products and the restricted area available for grain cultivation were responsible for further growth in feed grain imports, and in 1964 Japan became the largest U. S. market for feed grains. Altogether, 570 million bushels of corn and 148 million of sorghum left American ports for overseas markets in fiscal 1965.

In 1966, through a combination of circumstances, the feed grain needs of importing countries leaped by almost 300 million bushels, or about 20 percent above those of the previous year, and the United States was able to supply virtually all of the increased requirements. The Common Market alone accounted for almost one-half of the increase, mainly because of reduced grain harvests and insufficient stocks. Spain registered the next largest increase, more than 60 million bushels, brought about by reduced production as well as expanded requirements. This, as we have seen, was the year when world stocks of wheat were sharply down from previous levels, and much of the world experienced great concern over the adequacy of present and future food supplies. It was also the year when severe drought drastically cut India's grain production, raising her import needs to record proportions. Fortunately, many Indians were accustomed to eating sorghum, and shipments of 40 million bushels of this grain from the United States constituted an acceptable substitute during the emergency.[4]

By the end of the crop year in September, 1966, total American exports had reached 687 million bushels of corn, 266 million of sorghum, and 77 million of barley. Exports of oats, at 37 million bushels, had also marked the second highest volume of the postwar period. These figures represented all-time record levels of exports, and in fact, the period following the 1966 peak was one of appreciable decline in American feed grain exports, due primarily to the prevalence of political over economic considerations in a number of countries on both the export and import sides of the ledger.

While the United States was consistently the largest producer of corn, with total crops larger than the combined harvests of Europe, Africa, Asia, Oceania, and South America, other countries such as France, Thailand, and Brazil emerged for the first time in the 1960s as surplus producers of this principal feed grain. Considering all feed grains together, just nine countries—the

United States, Canada, Argentina, South Africa, Australia, Mexico, Thailand, Brazil, and France- -accounted for 80 to 90 percent of world feed grain exports during a decade in which world trade in these commodities almost doubled, going from almost 900 million to 1.7 billion bushels. The United States' share was 50 percent of the total in 1960, and rose to more than 55 percent in the peak year of 1966. But by July, 1967, the five-year phase-in period for achieving a Common Agricultural Policy was completed in the six Common Market countries, and the damaging consequences for American feed grain exports were quickly felt. The United States' share of world feed grain exports dropped to about 40 percent, a level around which it would remain for the next two years, while the share of the other eight main exporters rose to almost 50 percent. France, which in 1960 had exported only about 20 million bushels of corn and barley, shipped almost 250 million in 1969, mostly but not entirely in intra-Common Market trade. Altogether, from 1960 to 1969 production of feed grains in the Common Market increased by 37 percent, while imports of feed grains from third countries, which had increased 69 percent during the same period, fell by 1969 to only 24 percent more than they had been in 1960. Meanwhile, Common Market exports of feed grains to third countries, aided by large export subsidies, increased sixfold during the 1960s, while production also continued to increase under the stimulus of high domestic support prices and behind the shield of high levels of import protection. There was also a sharp rise in the use of other feed ingredients, such as high protein meals and beet pulp, to the detriment of feed grain consumption. Also, to further reduce net Common Market imports of feed grains, wheat was increasingly used for feed in the Community, and, again with high subsidies and after denaturing, exported in very sizable volume.

The decline in the use of American feed grains in the late 1960s was not limited to the Common Market. In Spain the U. S. share of the market, which had generally hovered around one-half, dropped to less than 10 percent in 1969, mainly as a result of competition from Argentine, Brazilian, and French corn. Furthermore, following surplus production of wheat, which had to be dumped into the world market at heavy losses, Spain by the end of the decade began switching wheat land to feed grain cultivation, both to achieve a better balance in wheat production and to further reduce her needs for imported feed grains. The

United Kingdom, a major importer of corn primarily from the United States, was a relatively static market during the 1960s, but Britain's imminent entry into the Common Market cast an ominous shadow on the prospects of continued marketing advantage for American corn over French.

In a concerted effort to regain lost ground, the U.S.D.A.'s Foreign Agricultural Service and a number of trade groups intensified the promotional efforts which they had cooperatively carried out through the 1960s in more than seventy foreign countries. Teams composed of representatives of the producers, the exporters, and the U. S. government, visited country after country to meet importers and manufacturers and stress the competitive availability of American supplies. In some countries, publicity campaigns were launched, aiming at increased awareness of the desirability of American feeding methods and ingredients. In Japan, for instance, a joint drive by the U. S. Feed Grains Council and Japanese groups, emphasizing the latest technical developments to the Japanese feed and poultry industry, made consumers more aware of the importance of eggs and poultry in the diet. This brought about an increase in egg consumption from 144 eggs per capita in 1963 to 214 in 1968, while Japanese poultry consumption also underwent a spectacular expansion, thus boosting demand for feed grains.[5]

The closing year of the decade thus marked a relative resurgence of American feed grain exports, with the United States' share of world trade climbing back to 46 percent of the total. Corn and sorghum were mainly responsible for the improvement, since American exports of barley and oats represented only very small proportions of total world trade; actually the United States participation in 1969-70 amounted to more than half of total corn exports and almost two-thirds of the world trade in sorghum.

The improvement did not come from the Common Market, which, in fact, sharply reduced its net imports to the lowest levels since 1957, while boosting its domestic production as well as its exports with the help of import protection, high internal support prices, and heavy export subsidies.

Some of the increased demand for American corn and sorghum in 1970 came from Mexico, which, hit by reduced harvests caused by a prolonged drought, switched from its normal position of corn exporter to that of being a net importer. However, the bulk of the higher demand once again came from Japan, which accounted for 180 million bushels of corn and almost **80 million** bushels of sorghum.

Despite the fact that the next year the corn crop was reduced to 4.1 billion bushels by the southern corn leaf blight, and corn exports therefore declined to 500 million bushels, prompt action in the use of blight-resistant seed and favorable atmospheric conditions pointed to a quick resumption of growth for American corn harvests.

Thus, at the threshold of the 1970s, the United States stood poised to expand further her exports of feed grains, with the certainty that her superior productive capacity and efficiency would permit such expansion if allowed to proceed on competitive terms. The problem was clearly defined at this time by an official of the U. S. Department of Agriculture, who, after exhorting American producers of corn and sorghum to consider overseas markets as important as domestic outlets, stated:

World trade policy and the domestic agricultural policies of various countries are at a critical point in their history. The world's nations could go either way—toward more protectionism or to more liberalism in their trade policies. This is a key question, not only in terms of world trade, but also in relation to future economic development of countries that need to trade in order to develop. So we need all the help we can muster to move the world toward more liberal trade policies.[6]

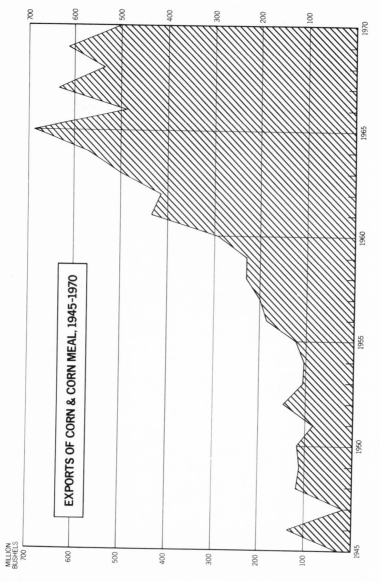

Fig. 9. (Source: United States Department of Agriculture, **Agricultural Statistics** (Washington, D. C.: United States Printing Office, 1967, 1970, 1971)).

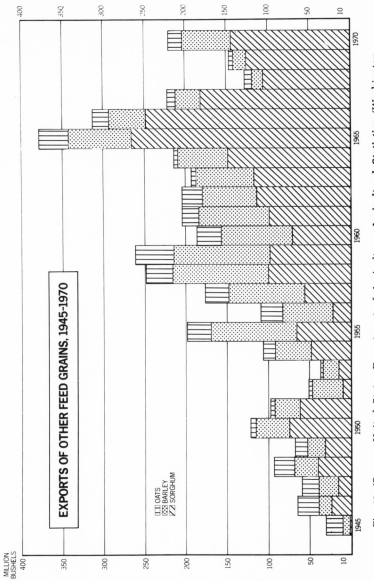

Fig. 10. (Source: United States Department of Agriculture, **Agricultural Statistics** (Washington. D. C.: United States Printing Office, 1967, 1970, 1971)).

TABLE 14—CORN STATISTICS,

Year Beginning Oct. 1	ACREAGE		Yield Per Harvested Acre (bus. per a.)	Production for grain (mill. bus.)
	Total Planted (mill. a.)	Harvested for grain (mill. a.)		
1945	89.2	77.9	33.1	2,577
1946	88.9	78.4	37.2	2,916
1947	85.0	73.8	28.6	2,108
1948	85.5	76.8	43.0	3,307
1949	86.7	77.1	38.2	2,946
1950	82.8	72.4	38.2	2,764
1951	83.3	72.2	36.9	2,629
1952	82.2	71.3	41.8	2,981
1953	81.6	70.7	40.7	2,882
1954	82.2	68.7	39.4	2,708
1955	80.9	68.5	42.0	2,873
1956	77.8	64.9	47.4	3,075
1957	73.2	63.1	48.3	3,045
1958	73.3	63.5	52.8	3,356
1959	82.7	72.1	53.1	3,825
1960	81.4	71.4	54.7	3,907
1961	65.9	57.6	62.4	3,598
1962	65.0	55.7	64.7	3,606
1963	68.8	59.2	67.9	4,019
1964	65.8	55.4	62.9	3,484
1965	65.1	55.3	73.8	4,084
1966	66.3	56.9	72.3	4,117
1967	71.0	60.6	78.6	4,760
1968	65.1	55.9	78.6	4,393
1969	64.2	54.6	83.9	4,578
1970	67.1	57.3	71.7	4,109

1945-1970

Total Domestic Use (Food, Feed, Seed, etc.) (mill. bus.)	Exports (mill. bus.)	Exports as Percentage of Production	SEASON'S AVERAGE PRICES	
			Received by Farmers ($ per bus.)	at Chicago (#3 Yellow) ($ per bus.)
2,690	31	1.20	1.23	1.94
2,670	136	4.66	1.53	1.80
2,554	15	.71	2.16	2.33
2,500	118	3.57	1.28	1.38
2,804	112	3.80	1.24	1.29
2,752	117	4.23	1.52	1.73
2,801	82	3.12	1.66	1.83
2,555	145	4.86	1.52	1.59
2,628	104	3.61	1.48	1.53
2,491	103	3.80	1.43	1.48
2,624	120	4.18	1.35	1.24
2,638	184	5.98	1.29	1.31
2,797	200	6.57	1.11	1.21
3,072	230	6.85	1.12	1.21
3,333	230	6.01	1.05	1.17
3,387	292	7.47	1.00	1.10
3,527	435	12.09	1.10	1.11
3,479	416	11.54	1.12	1.19
3,348	500	12.44	1.11	1.20
3,305	570	16.36	1.17	1.26
3,705	687	16.82	1.16	1.27
3,648	487	11.83	1.24	1.36
3,789	633	13.30	1.03	1.12
3,907	536	12.20	1.08	1.17
4,086	612	13.37	1.16	1.25
	501	12.19	1.34	1.46

TABLE 15—OTHER FEED GRAINS—

Year Beginning Oct. 1	Production (mill. bu.)	SORGHUM			Avg. Price $ per bu.)	Production (mill. bu.)
		Domestic Use (mill. bu.)	Exports (mill. bu.)			
1945	96	95	1		1.20	267
1946	106	82	24		1.40	265
1947	93	76	17		1.83	282
1948	131	79	40		1.28	316
1949	148	75	32		1.13	237
1950	334	181	75		1.05	304
1951	163	129	62		1.32	257
1952	91	84	10		1.58	228
1953	116	86	15		1.32	247
1954	236	135	48		1.26	379
1955	243	171	66		.98	403
1956	205	185	22		1.15	377
1957	568	281	57		.97	443
1958	581	386	100		1.00	477
1959	555	396	98		.86	420
1960	620	428	71		.84	429
1961	480	422	99		1.01	392
1962	510	403	113		1.02	428
1963	585	484	117		.98	393
1964	490	425	148		1.05	386
1965	673	582	266		1.00	392
1966	715	614	248		1.03	393
1967	756	545	166		.99	373
1968	740	635	106		.95	423
1969	747	663	126		1.07	424
1970	697	708	144		1.13	410

STATISTICS, 1945-1970

BARLEY			OATS			
Domestic Use (mill. bu.)	Exports (mill. bu.)	Avg. Price ($ per bu.)	Production (mill. bu.)	Domestic Use (mill. bu.)	Exports (mill. bu.)	Avg. Price ($ per bu.)
300	9	1.01	1,524	1,471	21	.65
256	16	1.38	1,478	1,469	26	.80
263	24	1.73	1,176	1,249	21	1.04
251	28	1.16	1,450	1,336	25	.72
254	22	1.06	1,220	1,306	16	.66
264	40	1.19	1,369	1,314	7	.79
260	31	1.26	1,278	1,344	5	.82
238	37	1.37	1,217	1,310	4	.79
246	19	1.17	1,153	1,252	3	.74
300	43	1.09	1,410	1,339	15	.71
342	103	.92	1,496	1,427	29	.60
332	62	.99	1,151	1,247	27	.69
333	92	.89	1,290	1,203	28	.60
347	117	.90	1,401	1,330	32	.58
349	118	.86	1,050	1,106	45	.65
373	86	.84	1,153	1,068	29	.60
357	84	.98	1,010	1,038	21	.64
343	67	.92	1,012	995	24	.62
349	71	.90	965	925	6	.62
369	61	.95	852	886	5	.63
318	77	1.02	927	854	37	.62
338	45	1.05	801	831	20	.67
334	31	1.00	789	779	10	.66
359	13	.91	939	831	8	.60
382	17	.87	949	832	5	.59
412	59	.92	909	840	17	.62

Notes To Chapter VI

1. Murray R. Benedict and Oscar C. Stine, *The Agricultural Commodity Programs—Two Decades of Experience* (New York: Twentieth Century Fund, 1956), p. 185.
2. This and all subsequent statistical data in the chapter are drawn from: United States Department of Agriculture, *Agricultural Statistics* (Washington, D.C.: United States Printing Office, 1967, 1970, 1971).
3. Benedict and Stine, *The Agricultural Commodity Programs,* p. 229.
4. Larry F. Thomasson, "The Story of the 1960's: U. S. Feed Grains in World Trade," *Foreign Agriculture,* Vol. III, No. 3 (January 19, 1970), p. 5.
5. Clarence D. Palmby, "The World Feed Situation in the 1970's," *Foreign Agriculture,* Vol. VII, No. 24 (June 16, 1969), p. 2.
6. Clarence D. Palmby, "Changes Shaping World Feedgrain Trade," *Foreign Agriculture,* Vol. VIII, No. 5 (February 2, 1970), p. 4.

VII

1945-1970 The Soybean Explosion

The meteoric rise of the soybean on the agricultural export scene has been described as a typical American success story—the immigrant starting out by performing the lowliest tasks and eventually, through versatility and intrinsic worth, rising to wealth and prominence.

For the soybean the "old country" was China, where, according to ancient Chinese literature, soybeans were extensively cultivated and highly valued both as food and as a source of medical remedies as early as 3000 B.C. By the early eighteenth century they had been introduced into Europe, where they were merely regarded as a curiosity in botanical gardens. Then, in 1804, a few bags arrived in the United States as part of the reserve food stocks of a Yankee Clipper, and by the middle of the century soybeans were being sparsely grown in the warmer sections of the country exclusively as forage. During the Civil War roasted and ground soybeans were sometimes used to brew a substitute for coffee.

Soybeans were in no way a factor in world trade until the beginning of the twentieth century, and their emergence was actually due to a fortuitous historical event. During the Sino-Japanese War of 1895, production of soybeans was vastly increased in Manchuria to feed the Japanese troops there, with the result that at war's end a soybean surplus developed. Then, as immigration restrictions were relaxed, masses of Chinese farmers moved into Manchuria, increasing cultivation still further, while Japan, which had acquired treaty rights in that region after her victory over Russia in 1905, began an extensive export trade in soybeans and oil with Europe.

In the United States, until after World War I, soybeans were grown almost exclusively for hay and forage, except for the small harvesting needed to provide seed. During the war, however, the United States experienced a serious shortage of fats and oils, which was in part relieved by the importation of Manchurian soybean oil; significantly, the first soybean statistic was published

131

BREAD UPON THE WATERS

by the U. S. Department of Agriculture in 1919, reporting that 99,000 acres had been planted with soybeans during that year.[1]

For the next fifteen years, although acreage continued to expand constantly and dramatically, soybeans were still grown primarily for hay, or, since they absorb nitrogen directly from the atmosphere, plowed back into the soil in order to fertilize it. About one-fourth of the planted acreage was harvested for beans, which were then pressed into meal for livestock feeding and oil to be used in soaps, paints, varnishes, and other industrial products.

The big breakthrough came in the mid-1930s, with the development of refining processes which were able to remove from the oil its inherently unpalatable flavor and odor, and thus make it usable for the production of margarine, shortening, and other products for human consumption. Production of soybean oil, which in the United States had slowly climbed from 2 million pounds in 1924 to 78 million ten years later, skyrocketed to 209 million pounds in 1935, and by the outbreak of World War II in 1939 it had reached 533 million pounds.[2]

Production of soybeans, which in 1931 was 17 million bushels, by 1939 had reached 90 million bushels without the need of any government price support and despite the fact that, since soybeans were classified as a soil depleting crop when harvested for beans, there had been some government attempts to limit acreage expansion. Exports of soybeans, although some small quantities had been shipped abroad since 1931, were not reported as a separate export commodity until 1938, when 4 million bushels were exported. The next year exports rose to 11 million bushels. The beginning of hostilities in Europe put an end to this promising foreign trade development, but at the same time strongly stimulated United States production of soybeans and consumption of their products to replace other oil and feed supplies which might be cut off by the war. As the flow of imports from traditional world sources in fact diminished, Washington in 1941 inaugurated the first price support program for soybeans, which, however, did not result in any accumulation in government hands as prices remained above loan levels despite increased production.

Then, in January, 1942, the secretary of agriculture announced the lifting of all restrictions on acreage and urged further expansion, with the assurance that soybean prices would be supported through the war period and for two years thereafter. Support for the 1942 crop was set at $1.60 a bushel. Under this stimulus, the 1942 soybean crop was almost 75 percent larger than that of 1941, reaching a total of 187 million bushels. From the soybeans that were processed, 1.2 billion pounds of oil and 3.2 million tons of meal were produced. Production continued at around these volumes for the rest of the war years, helped by increases in the support level to $1.80 for the 1943 crop and to $2.04 for the following two years. Since price ceilings had been placed on soybean products soon after Pearl Harbor, by 1943 support levels for soybeans were well above what processors could pay and still sell the products at ceiling prices, but Washington solved the impasse by contracting with the processors to buy beans at support prices for account of the government, and then selling them back to the processors at lower prices in line with ceilings.[3]

After decontrol in October, 1946, soybean prices advanced sharply and for the next two years remained far above support levels, since the harvesting of a record crop of 203 million bushels in 1946-47 had been followed in 1947-48 by lower yields resulting in reduced production.

In the first postwar years, the opportunities for expanding foreign trade in American soybeans and products were clearly visible. China, which had been the world's largest soybean shipper, was torn by internal strife and her production and trade were disrupted. Japan, which had previously drawn her supplies from Manchuria, was now cut off from that source, and badly in need of all foodstuffs. And Europe, just embarking on the road to economic recovery, and with her industrial plants in shambles, urgently required not only grain but also oils, fats, and animal feed.

In the first three peacetime years, United States exports included virtually no soybeans, although some quantities of soybean oil and meal were shipped abroad. But by 1948-49 the United States, which before the war had normally imported about 40 percent of her requirements of fats and oils, had become a net exporter of oils, oilseeds, and protein meals, thanks primarily to her expanded cultivation and use of soybeans, which, not undeservedly, were and are called "the miracle crop."

No other farm product is as versatile as the soybean. In a variety of food products, soybeans constitute the major source of protein in the diet of the population of Japan and other Asian countries, and are increasingly used by many western nations to supplement and increase the nutritive value of many food items. The oil which is extracted from soybeans, about 10.5 pounds from each bushel, is used not only in the production of shortening, margarine, and salad dressing, but also in cosmetics, confectionery, resins, and a myriad other uses, more of which are constantly being discovered. The oil contains lecithin, a compound with nutritional as well as emulsifying properties. The fatty acids derived from soybean oil are important components in detergents, soaps, plasticizers, and paints. In addition, the meal ground from the soybean meats remaining after the oil has been extracted—about forty-eight pounds for each bushel—has a protein content of almost 46 percent. Prior to the development of formula feeds, soybean meal had had difficulty gaining acceptance, since few knew how to use such a high protein ingredient. As feed mills developed sophisticated formulations, however, soybean meal quickly became a most valuable source of concentrated protein for poultry as well as other livestock.

Given these exceptional qualities of usefulness and versatility, it was only natural that the demand for soybeans both domestically and from abroad should increase sharply and consistently, finally raising them in only two decades to the number one spot among American agricultural exports.

The first significant exporting of soybeans took place in 1948-49, which marked the turning point in the United States switching from the status of an importer of oilseeds, oils, and fats, to that of a net exporter. That year 23 million bushels of soybeans were shipped abroad together with 300 million pounds of oil and 151,000 tons of meal. During the rest of the decade and the early 1950s, exports of soybeans and products fluctuated somewhat, although maintaining an upward trend. Then, in 1954-55, the soybean harvest hit the record level of 341 million bushels, of which 60 million were exported, or almost double the average of the preceding five years, while 249 million were crushed by American oil mills, again an all-time high.

The main reason for the expansion of production was the growing demand for soybean meal by the American livestock industry. The crushing industry, however, was faced with the perennial problem of disposing of the oil, which was and sometimes still is less in the demand than the meal, but which is nevertheless inevitably produced when soybeans are crushed. The problem was enhanced by the fact that processing of soybeans was no longer done by mechanical means, but increasingly and ultimately exclusively by treating the flaked soybeans with solvents, which extracted virtually their entire oil contents. Here, too, the implementation of PL 480 provided the solution. Beginning in 1955, as American production of soybeans grew by leaps and bounds, and domestic crush and utilization of meal followed apace, increasing quantities of soybean oil, ranging from 500 to 900 million pounds yearly for the rest of the decade, were sold for payment in foreign currency or donated for welfare distribution to a lengthening list of countries, from Spain and Italy to Yugoslavia and Poland, North African and Middle Eastern nations, Latin American ones, and eventually Pakistan and India.

Meanwhile, as the industrialized countries of northwestern Europe continued to increase their livestock and poultry numbers, their crushing industries turned more and more to American soybeans as the oilseed which, when compared to others, resulted in the largest percentage of high protein meal and the smallest of oil. Furthermore, since the nutritive value of a given meal largely reflects its crude protein content as well as its digestibility and quality, the latter depending mainly on amino acid composition, soybean meal with its high protein content, relatively high amino acid balance, and high coefficient of digestibility, could be used in feeding all classes of livestock, and consequently gained increasingly wide acceptance.[4]

Thus not only exports of soybeans rose, from 67 million bushels in 1955-56 to 85 the next year and 141 million in the closing year of the decade, but also exports of meal increased, from 400,000 tons in 1955 to 649,000 five years later.

The first half of the 1960s saw sharp and dramatic increases in every aspect of soybean production and utilization. The acres planted and bushels harvested went from 24.4 million acres and 555 million bushels in 1960-61 to 35.2 million acres and 845 million bushels in 1965-66. During the same period, while over 1 billion pounds of oil were shipped abroad each year, mostly with PL 480 financing, exports of soybeans doubled, from 130 to 250 million bushels, and exports of soybean meal, going from 590,000 to 2.6 million tons, registered an increase of more than 400 percent.

This tremendous expansion was the result of sustained demand both at home and abroad, and it should be noted that promotional programs instituted in a number of foreign countries by such

135

organizations as the Soybean Council of America and the American Soybean Association, in cooperation with the U.S.D.A.'s Foreign Agricultural Service, had a vital role in developing new acceptance for American soybeans and their products.

While, for instance, Germany, the Netherlands, Formosa, and Japan were traditional users of soybeans, and market expansion there resulted from natural growth in consumption volume due to population increases, other countries such as Spain, Italy, and France had not in the past been engaged in large-scale scientific poultry raising, and their populations, accustomed to the taste of olive and peanut oils, generally disliked soybean oil. Eventually, however, resistance was largely overcome, and not only did Spain for a period switch from the role of a PL 480 recipient to that of a dollar customer for sizable quantities of soybean oil, but all three countries vastly enlarged their crushing capacity and became very important buyers of American soybeans, both to supply meal to their burgeoning livestock industries and to produce salad oil.

The expansion also resulted in further enlargement of the soybean cultivation area. The cornbelt remained the principal growing zone, especially the states of Illinois, Iowa, and Indiana, but the attractive financial returns of soybean cultivation increasingly caused farmers in the Mississippi Delta to switch their land from cotton or timber to soybeans. Missouri, Mississippi and Arkansas became major producers, while the development of hardier varieties permitted soybean cultivation to extend northward into Minnesota.

Nineteen-sixty-six marked the beginning of a three-year period in which government intervention had a detrimental effect on the growth rate of American soybean exports. Until then, support prices had been set at levels which, while aimed at encouraging production, would keep it in line with domestic and foreign demand and prevent the accumulation of market-disrupting surpluses. As a result, a fine balance had been maintained, and while from time to time some quantities had been put under CCC loan they had eventually been redeemed. As of September, 1965, the Commodity Credit Corporation owned just nine thousand bushels of soybeans.

The next year the support price for soybeans was raised from $2.25 to $2.50 a bushel. As a result, acreage expanded excessively and production rose to 928 million bushels, more than was required for a yearly supply by domestic and foreign crushers and to keep stocks in transit to them at normal levels.

A similar situation prevailed in 1967 and 1968, and in the latter year, on an unprecedented 42 million acres and because of a record yield of 26.8 bushels per acre, American farmers raised their first billion bushel crop of soybeans; in fact, the total harvest amounted to 1,103 million bushels.

Exports, during the 1966-1968 period, remained relatively stationary, while a growing mountain of soybeans accumulated in CCC inventories. By August, 1969, 150 million bushels of soybeans were owned by the Commodity Credit Corporation, and, as usual in such circumstances, their very existence weighed heavy on the market.

Realizing its earlier error, the U. S. Department of Agriculture brought the support level for 1969 back to $2.25 a bushel, and the effects were immediate and electrifying. On approximately the same acreage, an even larger crop was raised, 1,126 million bushels. However, with prices made more competitive, exports of soybeans in 1969-70 skyrocketed to 428 million bushels from the previous year's level of 286 million. At the same time, soybean meal exports, which had amounted to 3 million tons in 1968-69, jumped to 4 million tons. The following year the trend continued, with exports still higher at the all-time record levels of 433 million bushels of soybeans and 4.5 million tons of meal. Considering that it takes 40 million bushels of beans to produce one million short tons of meal, overseas shipments of soybeans and meal in 1969-70 represented a total of 612 million bushels, or almost 54 percent of total bean production. With a combined value of more than $1.5 billion, soybeans thus gained first place among American agricultural exports.

Although Japan was the largest single importer of soybeans throughout the 1960s, the combined imports of the Common Market countries were larger, and Europe as a whole generally accounted for more than one-half of American exports. A promising development, in the closing years of the decade, was the growing demand for soybeans as well as soybean meal on the part of Eastern European countries, such as Bulgaria, Hungary, Yugoslavia, Poland, and Czechoslovakia. An ominous sign, on the other hand, was consideration by the Common Market in 1969 of the imposition of an internal consumption tax on oils and protein meals, which could not fail to have detrimental effects on American exports of soybeans and their products.

Still, as American soybeans entered their fourth decade of major production expansion and their third of explosive export development, the outlook for further growth in demand and utilization both at home and abroad was brightly promising. In a very brief time span, the immigrant had indeed "made good."

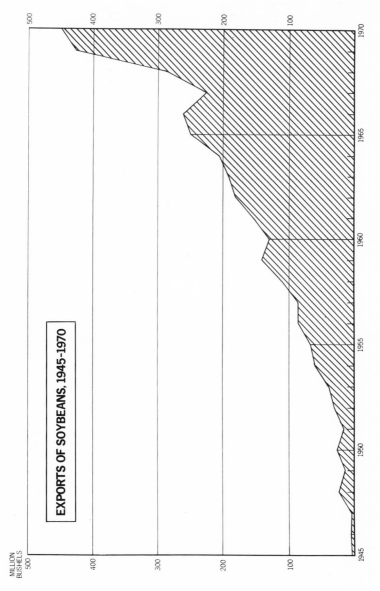

Fig. 11. (Source: United States Department of Agriculture, **Agricultural Statistics** (Washington, D. C.: United States Printing Office, 1967, 1970, 1971)).

TABLE 16—SOYBEAN STATISTICS,

Year Beginning October 1	ACREAGE Grown for all Purposes (mill. a.)	Harvested for Beans (mill. a.)	Yield per acre (bu. per a.)	Production (mill. bu.)	Domestic Crush (mill. bu.)	EXPORTS Beans (mill. bu.)	Oil (mill. lbs.)
1945	13.1	10.7	18.0	193.2	159.5	2.8	74
1946	11.7	9.9	20.5	203.4	170.2	3.8	89
1947	13.1	11.4	16.3	186.5	161.4	2.9	112
1948	12.0	10.7	21.3	227.2	183.7	23.0	300
1949	11.9	10.5	22.3	234.2	195.3	13.1	291
1950	15.0	13.8	21.7	299.3	252.0	27.8	490
1951	15.2	13.6	20.8	283.8	244.4	17.0	271
1952	16.0	14.4	20.7	298.9	234.4	31.9	93
1953	16.4	14.8	18.2	269.2	213.2	39.7	71
1954	18.5	17.0	20.0	341.1	249.0	60.6	50
1955	19.7	18.6	20.1	373.7	283.1	67.5	556
1956	21.7	20.6	21.8	449.3	315.9	85.4	807
1957	21.9	20.9	23.2	483.4	353.8	85.5	804
1958	25.1	24.0	24.2	580.2	401.2	110.1	930
1959	23.3	22.6	23.5	532.9	393.4	141.4	953
1960	24.4	23.7	23.5	555.1	402.2	130.1	721
1961	27.8	27.0	25.1	678.6	438.8	153.2	1,308
1962	28.4	27.6	24.2	669.2	474.5	180.3	1,165
1963	29.5	28.6	24.4	699.2	440.9	191.2	1,106
1964	31.6	30.8	22.8	700.9	473.1	205.9	1,357
1965	35.2	34.5	24.5	845.6	542.4	250.6	948
1966	37.3	36.6	25.4	928.5	566.1	261.6	1,105
1967	40.8	39.8	24.5	976.1	572.4	226.6	993
1968	42.0	41.1	26.8	1,103.1	615.2	286.8	899
1969	42.2	41.0	27.5	1,126.3	743.1	428.7	1,449
1970	43.3	42.4	26.8	1,135.8	775.0	433.2	1,736

1945-1970

AVERAGE PRICES

Meal (1000 tons)	Exports of Beans as perc. of Prod.	Exports of Beans and Meal as perc. of Bean Prod.	Received by Farmers ($ per bu.)	Beans (#2 Yellow at Chicago) ($ per bu.)	Oil (Crude Midwest) (¢ per lb.)	Meal (44% Protein Bulk, Decatur) ($ per ton of 2000 lbs.)
1	1.45	1.45	2.08	2.13	11.9	55.25
142	1.87	4.67	2.57	3.04	22.9	72.30
96	1.55	3.59	3.33	3.80	23.8	80.80
151	10.12	12.76	2.27	2.45	13.1	66.10
47	5.59	6.40	2.16	2.29	12.3	64.30
181	9.29	11.69	2.47	2.61	17.8	64.45
42	5.99	6.59	2.73	2.98	11.3	83.35
47	10.67	11.31	2.72	2.88	12.1	67.55
67	14.75	15.75	2.72	2.71	13.5	78.65
272	17.77	20.96	2.46	2.77	11.9	60.70
400	18.06	22.34	2.22	2.40	12.5	52.55
443	19.01	22.95	2.18	2.34	12.7	47.45
300	17.69	20.17	2.07	2.24	10.8	53.40
512	18.98	22.51	2.00	2.14	9.5	55.80
649	26.53	31.41	1.96	2.16	8.3	55.55
590	23.44	27.69	2.13	2.17	11.3	60.60
1,064	22.58	30.28	2.28	2.43	9.5	63.60
1,476	26.94	35.76	2.34	2.54	8.9	71.25
1,478	27.35	35.78	2.51	2.74	8.5	71.00
2,036	29.38	40.99	2.62	2.82	11.4	70.20
2,602	29.64	41.95	2.54	2.63	11.8	81.50
2,657	28.17	39.73	2.75	2.92	10.1	78.80
2,899	23.21	35.10	2.49	2.64	8.4	76.90
3,044	26.00	37.04	2.43	2.56	8.3	74.10
4,035	38.06	52.39	2.35	2.68	11.0	78.40
4,487	38.15	53.92	2.84	2.98	12.82	78.56

Notes To Chapter VII

1. "The Soybean and ASA—Fifty Years of Growing Up Together," *Foreign Agriculture,* Vol. III, No. 46 (November 16, 1970), p. 3.

2. This and all subsequent statistical data in the chapter are drawn from: United States Department of Agriculture, *Agricultural Statistics* (Washington, D.C.: United States Printing Office, 1967, 1970, 1971).

3. Benedict and Stine, *The Agricultural Commodity Programs,* pp. 169-172.

4. "U. S. Meal and Oil in World Trade," *Foreign Agriculture,* Vol. VIII, No. 7 (February 16, 1970), p. 3.

Emptying threshed wheat from a combine in a field near Fargo,
North Dakota, for hauling to a local grain elevator in August,
1945.

(United States Department of Agriculture)

A skilled farm hand operates a single-row corn picker in a field
near Hummelstown, Dauphin County, Pennsylvania in November, 1947.

(United States Department of Agriculture)

Shelling corn on a farm in Phillips County, Colorado, in May, 1947.
(United States Department of Agriculture)

Lacking storage bins, Sherman County, Kansas, farmers in 1925 left part of their crop in piles on the ground until they could arrange to haul it to market.
(United States Department of Agriculture)

Bunge Corporation's river elevator at Greenville, Mississippi.

At the peak of the surplus accumulation in the 1950's, wheat was stored in special tents designed to provide supplemental storage for Commodity Credit Corporation grain. The ones shown here, at St. Joseph, Missouri, held about one million bushels each.

(United States Department of Agriculture)

Greenville, Mississippi. As one loaded barge is pushed off, an empty one is maneuvered under the end of the loading spout.

At the junction of the Mississippi and Ohio Rivers at Cairo, Illinois, three Bunge facilities collect grain for movement to seaboard.

(Swoboda, Shelton & Moreland, Cairo, Illinois)

A major inland terminal elevator. Note in the center the railcar unloading tunnels.
(Anderson Photo Company, Kansas City, Missouri)

The main grain elevator at Galveston, Texas.
(Brad Messer Photography, Galveston, Texas)

Savage, Minnesota. Concrete and steel storage tanks with a capacity of more than six million bushels, and the rail car unloading area.

Savage, Minnesota—Start of a 1693 mile trip! Shortly after this barge—the first one loaded at Port Bunge in April, 1967—was filled with soybeans, it left for Destrehan, Louisiana, where Bunge Corporation operates an eight million bushel export elevator. The special movable tripper system on the loading dock speeds loading of barges.

Trading floor of the Chicago Board of Trade taken from the boardmarkers catwalk at the west end of the floor. In the immediate foreground is a telephone bank; beyond that the futures traders in the soybean pit. In the background, from left, the corn, oats and wheat pits are also visible. At far left are a few tables of the cash grain market, and at the top of the picture are the quotation boards at the east end of the trading floor.
(Joseph J. Lugas, Jr., Chicago, Illinois)

A close-up of floor traders in action.
(Joseph J. Lugas, Jr., Chicago, Illinois)

Port Bunge, Minnesota. A fully loaded trailer truck is hydrauli-
cally lifted to dump its cargo into the pit from which the grain
will be conveyed into the elevator.

As far as the eye can see, rows of maturing soybean plants
cover the rich Missouri soil.

East St. Louis, Illinois, January, 1971. A tugboat is shown pushing a tow of grain-laden barges through the icy waters of the
Mississippi River. Tows of up to 30 barges travel the river. Each
barge holds 75,000 bushels of grain.
(United States Department of Agriculture)

Loading grain in barges at East St. Louis, Illinois, September, 1959. Grain pouring from spout into barge.
(United States Department of Agriculture)

With their helicopter parked on an adjacent barge on the tow, inspectors from the Illinois Department of Agriculture sample grain from a barge traveling down the Mississippi River near East St. Louis, Illinois.
(United States Department of Agriculture)

Grain inspectors with the Illinois Department of Agriculture fill
bags with grain samples they have pulled from a barge on the
Mississippi River near East St. Louis, Illinois, January 20, 1971.
The grain will be carried with the inspectors by helicopter from
the barge to a lab for analysis.

(United States Department of Agriculture)

Wheat from one of Duluth's big grain elevators being loaded in
1945 into a Great Lakes freighter to be carried to Buffalo, N. Y.,
where some was milled and some transshipped through the
New York State Barge Canal to the port of New York and thence
overseas.

(United States Department of Agriculture)

The laker A. T. Kinney is shown in July, 1960, loading corn at the Gateway Elevator in Chicago.
(United States Department of Agriculture)

In June, 1941, barges haul Ever Normal Granary corn through the New York State Barge Canal to Albany, a center of distribution for the Grain League Federation Exchange, the first farmer cooperative to participate in the plan for storing reserve supplies of milled feed on farms in the East.
(United States Department of Agriculture)

Lake Charles, Louisiana, September, 1958. Milled rice in 100 pound sacks is brought from Lake Charles Port Storage to the docks on wooden platforms and then moved from the docks into the hold of the ship in a loading net operated by a large crane.
(United States Department of Agriculture)

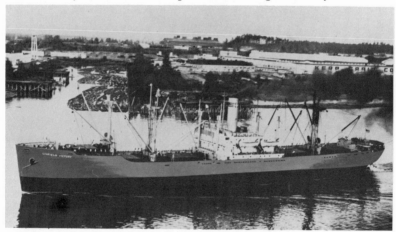

The Linfield Victory, typical of the thousands of cargo vessels built by U. S. shipyards during World War II.
(United States Maritime Administration)

Aerial view showing a section of the National Defense Reserve
Fleet anchored at Jones Point on the Hudson River, New York.
(United States Maritime Administration)

Grain transported from the Midwest in unit trains of 40 to 70
100-ton hopper cars leased by the Commodity Credit Corporation of the U. S. Department of Agriculture is loaded into a ship
at Baltimore, Maryland, in February, 1966. The crewmen are
preparing to seal the hatches. The CCC leased the trains to speed
the movement of grain to India. The Indian Government leased
the ship.
(United States Department of Agriculture)

The *Manhattan*, the U. S. largest tanker at the time, taking on U. S. wheat at Longview, Washington, December 29, 1966. The vessel, almost twice the length of the 555-foot Washington Monument, carried about 100,000 tons—the largest single shipment of U. S. wheat ever made to India. The first employment of the *Manhattan* as a grain carrier was made by Bunge Corporation in August, 1963, when it loaded on it at Destrehan, Louisiana, 75,000 tons of wheat for Pakistan.
(United States Department of Agriculture)

While a stevedore controls electronically the spout's movement, wheat pours into the *Manhattan*'s deep tanks.
(United States Department of Agriculture)

VIII

Portrait of An Exporter

Grain exporting today is perhaps the most competitive field in the entire business arena. Advertising may promote sales of a particular brand of cigarettes or toothpaste, and superior performance may gain preference for a make of automobiles or television sets. But wheat is wheat and corn is corn, and as long as the same grade requirements are fulfilled, the only way for an exporter to sell his grain is to offer it at a price lower than that of his competitors, the difference generally being a minute fraction of a cent per bushel. Today's instant communication facilities, furthermore, keep both American farmers and foreign buyers continuously and simultaneously informed of price fluctuations on the commodity exchanges and in the cash markets in the United States and in other exporting countries, while exporters in turn are made aware of each competitor's offers, of actual and potential demand, and of buyers' price ideas. As a result, the exporter's margin of profit does not, as a rule, come from a spread between prices paid and prices received for grain on equal terms, but, rather, as partial compensation for the performance of a multitude of functions such as accumulation, storage, transportation, financing, etc. Grain exporting, therefore, requires substantial fixed investment in elevator facilities as well as large working capital for the financing of grain stocks, and the number of firms in this field is consequently rather small. The grain trade is one field in which a man's word is still indeed his bond, where deals involving millions of dollars are concluded with one "yes" over the telephone, and no backtracking ever occurs between the oral agreement and the signing of a contract regardless of market price developments. In the United States at the present time there are about two dozen grain exporters, and, as it happens, they are all either marketing cooperatives or essentially privately owned companies. The major exporters are Cargill, Inc., and Peavey Company in Minneapolis, Continental Grain Co., Bunge Corporation, Louis Dreyfus & Co., and Garnac

Grain Co. in New York, Farmers Export Corporation in Kansas City, Cook & Co. in Memphis, and C. B. Fox & Co. in New Orleans. While there are differences in size and volume of business, the *modus operandi* of most exporters is basically similar.[1] Since a mere listing or technical description of the many functions performed by an exporter between the time grain is first acquired in the interior and its ultimate delivery to a buyer overseas would be an arid and probably boring recitation, the reader may instead obtain a more vivid and intelligible picture from a brief sketch of the history, organization, and daily operations of a major exporter, such as Bunge Corporation.

Bunge Corporation is just now celebrating its fiftieth anniversary, but its roots go back much farther. It was in 1818 that two Bunge brothers, members of a family that had been engaged in trading since the seventeenth century, founded in Amsterdam a firm dealing in commodities, primarily hides and spices, imported from Holland's overseas possessions. In 1850 the son of one of the founders, Charles Bunge, transferred the company's headquarters to Antwerp, and expanded its trading activities into grain, coffee, wool, and cotton. Charles had two sons, Edouard and Ernesto, both exceptionally gifted businessmen, who, each in his way and in different locales, shared in laying the groundwork for the eventual growth and success of the Bunge Group of Companies.

Edouard, as the elder, assumed the direction of the Belgian headquarters after Charles' death in 1884, and during his forty-three-year tenure as head of the firm he expanded commercial activities by establishing branches in Genoa, Hamburg, London, Paris, Copenhagen, and many other world trading centers. He was also instrumental, on behalf of King Leopold II of the Belgians, in establishing trading posts and organizing the export of tropical produce from the newly colonized territories of the Congo.

Ernesto Bunge, instead, emigrated to Buenos Aires in 1876, the very year when Argentina first emerged as a grain exporting country, and eight years later, together with his brother-in-law Jorge Born, set up Bunge & Born, Lda., an independent business which began shipping Argentine grain and other agricultural commodities to the Bunge houses and other customers in Europe and throughout the world.

As the Argentine company grew in volume and scope of business, it soon outstripped the Belgian one, with which close ties were nevertheless maintained. In 1897 Ernesto Bunge and Jorge Born were joined by Alfredo Hirsch, a brilliant young business-man who thirty years later would become the company's second president and hold that post for thirty years more. Under the leadership of Bunge, Born, and Hirsch, as well as their descend-ants and an elite cadre of rigorously selected and trained execu-tives, the Bunge Group expanded its activities in the international grain trade as well as in a vast array of industrial enterprises in Latin America, ranging from flour milling to oilseed crushing and the production and distribution of textiles, chemicals, containers, paints, and pharmaceuticals.

The Bunge Group's standard bearer in North America is Bunge Corporation, which today employs over twelve-hundred people and exports about a billion dollars worth of farm products a year.

Back in 1923, however, Bunge Corporation was but a fledgling member of the Group, created from the conversion of a small New York grain firm, P. N. Gray, Inc., originally formed by the Bunge Group in 1919.[2] It continued to operate on a relatively limited scale, both exporting and importing grain as well as other commodities, until the tremendous impulse given to American exports by the world-wide demand for grain and other food-stuffs at the end of World War II made it obvious that in order to compete successfully for a fair share of the business, Bunge would have to acquire storage facilities and engage in domestic as well as foreign grain trade.

A first step in that direction had been made in 1936 with the purchase of a terminal elevator in Minneapolis, followed by the acquisition of another large elevator in Fort Worth, Texas, in 1939. It was the year 1946, however, that marked the emergence of Bunge Corporation as a factor in domestic grain merchandising in the United States. This was accomplished through the acquisi-tion of two old and well-established companies, Gano Grain Co. of Hutchinson, Kansas, and Hallet & Carey Inc. of Minneapolis. Both of these firms owned and operated large terminal facilities as well as extensive lines of country elevators, and through them Bunge Corporation began its expansion into the grain-producing areas, in order ultimately to increase the efficiency of its export operations. It was a slow process, and in fact at this time Bunge was not in the forefront of the expansionary drive. The postwar leadership in organizing a capillary grain export organization was assumed by Cargill, Inc., and during the following decade that

Minneapolis-based firm built an extensive network of large and small elevators in the principal wheat and corn growing states, as well as export terminals on the lower Mississippi, the Atlantic Coast, and the St. Lawrence River.[3] Continental Grain Company of New York followed a similar, though somewhat less extensive, course of expansion and construction.

By the mid-1950s, therefore, when Bunge Corporation decided to embark on a major program of local grain purchasing and facility building, it was confronted with well-entrenched competition in the primary cereal producing areas. Furthermore, wheat and corn were at this time moving in ever increasing volume into CCC stocks, thus reducing the flow of these grains into private trade channels at the points of origin.

The one farm product which was not in surplus, which was consistently selling above support levels, and for which there was a steadily growing demand from overseas buyers, was soybeans, and it was to this crop that the first phase of Bunge's expansionary drive was geared. As soybean cultivation extended southward, replacing cotton in some areas and timber in other newly cleared ones, Bunge began erecting country elevators and subterminal facilities along navigable rivers, primarily the Mississippi, Ohio, Arkansas, White, Yazoo rivers. For speed and efficiency of handling, Bunge pioneered the storage of grain in large steel tanks, similar to those used for petroleum, but equipped with elevating and conveying machinery as well as provisions for aerating and conditioning the grain.

Having forged these new links in the chain connecting American farmers to overseas markets, the next step for Bunge was to become established at seaboard, a goal which was accomplished with the construction of a large terminal elevator at Destrehan, near New Orleans, and the long-term leasing of port facilities at Philadelphia, Galveston and Quebec.

Simultaneously, as marketing conditions improved in the corn and wheat belts with the gradual disappearance of CCC-held surpluses, Bunge expanded its activities at the origination level also in those areas, acquiring existing lines of country elevators as well as building additional facilities at focal river points. As an added outlet for American farm products, in 1967 Bunge built a large soybean crushing plant alongside its Destrehan elevator, from which soybean meal for cattle and poultry feeding and soybean oil for human consumption could be shipped directly to foreign destinations. Bunge Corporation's expansion was naturally paralleled by that of its main competitors, but the early lead taken in newly opened regions made it possible for Bunge to be consistently in the forefront of soybean exporters, while also accounting for very substantial exports of corn, sorghum, wheat, flaxseed and barley. Thus, thanks primarily to the successful implementation of its growth program during the 1960s, Bunge Corporation reached the half-century mark in its history as a major factor in United States agricultural exports.

As far as organizational structure is concerned, Bunge Corporation strives for a balanced mix of centralized policy controls and decentralized operations. The company's headquarters are in the Wall Street district of New York, and it is here that all export trading is conducted by tightly knit groups of specialists for each of the principal grains and for the other commodities sold by Bunge, primarily vegetable oils, animal fats, and protein feedstuffs. Through the use of leased wires and open teletype channels, as well as electronic quotation boards, the Bunge traders in New York are continuously aware of grain price fluctuations on the commodity exchanges in the United States and Canada and in the cash markets overseas, and they are in constant touch with other Bunge houses and independent sales agencies which, in turn, deal with buyers throughout the world.

The purchase, storage, and shipping of grain, as well as domestic merchandising, are handled by the various organizations through which Bunge Corporation operates on a regional basis: the Northwest Region, with headquarters in Minneapolis, the Atlantic Region, based in Philadelphia, the Southwest Region, centered in Kansas City, the River Grain Region, radiating southward from St. Louis, and the Destrehan Region, near New Orleans.

Each region operates and supervises a number of terminal and country elevators, either directly or through control of the districts into which the regions are further subdivided. Altogether Bunge Corporation owns and operates about 120 facilities, ranging from giant port terminals to small country elevators, with a total combined storage capacity well in excess of 100 million bushels. To better coordinate transportation of grain from the interior to seaboard, Bunge also owns and runs a fleet of more than 100 steel barges, each capable of carrying over 1,000 tons of grain.

How this organization functions in promoting the export of

American grain can perhaps best be seen by following a typical transaction from beginning to end.

On a weekday morning in February, for instance, one of the many cables delivered to the desk of John Muller, Bunge Vice-President in charge of soybean trading, is a request from Bunge G.m.b.H. in Hamburg for an offer of a large quantity of soybeans. The night before, as on every other night, Muller has cabled to Hamburg as well as to other Bunge houses in various countries the price at which they could sell, i.e., a price based on the closing quotations of Chicago soybean futures, plus a "basis" premium for delivering cash soybeans at seaboard, elevation, ocean freight, and insurance. On a distant shipping position, it should be noted, this "basis" premium is strictly a matter of opinion, but an exporter must have a price for any position a buyer may want to purchase, and it is here that the trader's judgment of crop forecasts and market projections comes into play. The overnight offers have permitted Hamburg to begin canvassing prospective buyers as soon as they opened for business, when it was still only 3:00 A.M. in New York. By now, however, it is daytime in the United States, the Chicago Board of Trade has begun operations, and the overnight offers are therefore no longer valid, while many European traders are getting ready to go home.

The inquiry the Bunge trader in Hamburg is transmitting comes from a multiplant oilseed crushing and margarine manufacturing industrial complex, whose buying committee has decided the market looks right for starting to buy forward supplies of raw materials. Specifically, they want to buy 20,000 metric tons of No. 2 yellow soybeans, for shipment to Rotterdam in December.

Cash soybeans for prompt shipment are selling at this time in New Orleans for $3.29 a bushel of sixty pounds, reflecting a "basis" premium of 12 cents a bushel over the nearest "futures" month on the Chicago Board of Trade, March. "New crop" soybeans have not even been planted yet—in the northern growing areas such as Illinois and Indiana, the ground is still frozen, while in the South many of the fields which will be planted to soybeans in May and June must first be harvested of the winter wheat growing on them.

To buy "old crop" beans and hold them until they could be shipped in December would make the price prohibitive since it would mean increasing their cost by the amount of carrying charges, such as storage, conditioning to avoid spoilage, and interest on tied-up money.

Obviously, therefore, Muller's offer must be of "new crop" soybeans, and such an offer is made possible by the existence and viability of the Chicago "futures" market. Looking up at the electronic quotation board which occupies an entire wall of the large trading room in which he sits with his assistants and his colleagues handling other types of grain, Muller sees that November soybeans are trading in Chicago at $3.07 a bushel. On this basis, after adding what he estimates will be the "cash premium" in the fall, what his colleagues in the Chartering Department expect to be a realistic rate of ocean freight next December (freight rates, after all, fluctuate just as grain prices do), and additional factors to cover stevedoring, insurance, quality inspection, selling commission and other handling charges, Muller calculates a price of $122.75 per metric ton, CIF Rotterdam. He telephones the Communications Department, asking that they get Bunge-Hamburg on the teletype, and by the time he walks down the corridor to the telex room, the connection has been made and his German colleague is standing by at the other end. After dictating to the teletype operator the terms and price of the offer, Muller in turn waits while the German trader contacts the prospective buyer by telephone. The answer soon comes back: the buyer has meanwhile received an offer from another exporter at $122.60 per ton, to which he has countered with a bid at $122.25. Should the bid not be accepted, is Bunge willing to sell at that price? Muller indicates that, given a chance to work the bid for a short time, he hopes to be able to accept it, and since presumably the other exporter has meanwhile declined it, the bid at $122.25 is now left with Bunge, with the stipulation that an answer must be received by the buyer within thirty minutes. Returning to his desk, Muller finds that November soybeans in Chicago have just traded down to $3.05¾ a bushel. He quickly reviews his calculations, revises slightly downward his estimate of the "cash basis," and decides that the business is feasible. At Muller's request, one of his assistants instructs the Bunge office in the Chicago Board of Trade to buy 735,000 bushels of November soybeans, a quantity equivalent to 20,000 metric tons. A few minutes later, through the direct telephone line linking his desk with the trading floor in Chicago, Muller is advised that the purchase of "futures" has been completed, and in turn he cables his confirmation of the sale to Hamburg for timely transmission to the buyer. The transaction, as far as Muller is concerned, is closed, since it is fully hedged, and he will not think about it anymore until new crop soybeans are harvested, several months later, or whenever farmers decide to start selling their new crop ahead of harvest.*

The scene now shifts in time to late October and in place to Osceola, Arkansas, a Bunge grain elevator on the bank of the Mississippi river about fifty miles north of Memphis.

It is late evening, but trailer trucks keep arriving from the fields loaded with soybeans just harvested. Gus Critz, a Bunge veteran who is manager of the Osceola elevator as well as of the district which covers four other river facilities, stands near the truck scale greeting the driver of the first rig, a middle-aged farmer with whom he has dealt for more than ten years. Outside the scale house, on a blackboard, is posted the price Gus is ready to pay for No. 1 soybeans—$3.20 a bushel. The Chicago closing price for November soybeans that afternoon has been $3.28, but that price represents No. 2 yellow soybeans in store in Chicago Board of Trade registered warehouses for delivery in November. Any soybeans Gus buys at the origination level must still be stored and moved to seaboard, and he must take into account the charges for this handling and transportation, as well as the cost of operating his elevator. The farmer is aware of these differentials, and he is also aware of the prices bid by other exporters, country elevators, and crushers in the area. With a handshake the deal is closed, and the unloading process begins.

First, a long tubular probe is inserted at various spots in the mound of ivory-colored, pea-sized soybeans filling the trailer, and the representative sample thus obtained is taken to the small laboratory adjoining the scale-house. While the sample is being tested for moisture, field damage, foreign matter, and other factors, the combination of which determines the grade and the scale of premiums and allowances under the basic price, a hydraulic

---

* In the above example, it appears that the foreign buyer, by purchasing at a flat price, is running the risk of market advance or decline. In actuality, he may simultaneously have hedged his purchase by forward sales of the meal and oil which will eventually be produced from the soybeans. Alternatively, with another technique which is increasingly being used by sophisticated European and Japanese buyers, the transaction might have involved negotiation and agreement only on a differential premium for cash soybeans CIF Rotterdam over Chicago futures, with the buyer's obligation to turn over to the seller a number of Chicago futures contracts equivalent to the tonnage of the soybeans physically shipped overseas.

piston tilts upwards the platform on which the trailer has been anchored after being weighed, and a golden avalanche cascades behind the scale into the dump pit from which the soybeans are moved through an underground conveyor to the elevator leg and thence into a large storage tank. By the time the truck is weighed empty, the exact grade has also been determined; the total value of the load is then quickly computed, and a few minutes later the farmer leaves with a Bunge check in his pocket. The next truck moves onto the scale, and the process is repeated, sometimes, if bad weather threatens to ruin the harvest, continuing through the night.

The following day, Gus Critz reports the total of his day's purchases to the headquarters of Bunge's River Grain Region in St. Louis, and the information is passed on to John Muller in New York. Muller must now begin to convert his long position of November soybean futures into cash soybeans with which to fulfill, among many others, the sale to Germany made eight months earlier. Over the next few days, as soybeans continue to arrive at river terminals, Muller buys them from Bunge's St. Louis office at the going market price, simultaneously selling out in Chicago equivalent quantities of November "futures." The market, owing to a number of factors, is substantially higher than it was back in February, but this does not affect the outcome of the transaction for Muller. True, he is paying an average of $3.40 a bushel for cash soybeans delivered FOB New Orleans, while his original selling price converted to only $3.18 a bushel; but the futures he bought at $3.06 are now worth $3.28, and what he is gaining on reselling them fully offsets his loss on the cash commodity.

It is now the beginning of November. As on every weekday afternoon, Muller attends a meeting at which Bunge's chief export grain traders discuss market conditions and developments, preliminary to the preparation and cabling of overnight offers. One of the subjects discussed at this daily meeting is the situation of the ocean freight market, and Muller is pleased to learn that there is no scarcity of ships seeking cargo for December lifting, and that freight rates from the Gulf of Mexico to Rotterdam are fifty cents per ton lower than what he calculated back in February. At Muller's request, Jerry Jenks, Bunge Vice-President in charge of freight chartering, contacts various ship brokers in New York and in London, and within a few days concludes the charter of the *New Haven,* a 23,000-ton ship which is at the moment en route from Japan to the United States with a cargo of steel plates, and which will be ready for loading grain at New Orleans around the middle of December. This vessel is thus earmarked for lifting the 20,000-ton sale, plus some others.

Meanwhile, at Osceola as well as at other river facilities, work is in progress to move the grain to seaboard. As a barge is maneuvered into position and made fast to the dock and pilings sunk deep into the riverbed a hundred feet offshore, electric motors start up and set in motion the conveyor belts and elevator legs through which the soybeans are moved from the bottom of the main storage tank out and up into smaller shipping bins, then out on the long gallery which extends over the water to the dock, and finally through a long tubular spout down into the boxlike steel barge. The end of the spout is frequently moved so that the load is well distributed and the barge maintains a level trim. When the barge is full, heavy steel covers slide into position on side rails, so that the cargo is well protected from the elements, and the full barge is shifted to a holding mooring while another takes its place under the loading spout. Every few days, just as railroad cars from many sidings are coupled together to form a train going to a common destination, Bunge's barges are picked up by a towboat and lashed to others coming from more northerly points. Then the entire tow, sometimes consisting of as many as twenty or more barges, slowly moves down the Mississippi toward New Orleans.

Fifteen miles north of New Orleans, behind a high levee on the left bank of the river, rises Bunge's Destrehan elevator, a massive concrete structure complemented by huge steel storage tanks and a hangarlike shed holding the soybean meal produced by the extraction plant behind the elevator. More than one hundred feet above the ground, a bridgelike structure on high steel trestles extends for almost eight-hundred feet from the headhouse over a highway, the levee, and a wide stretch of water, to rest on pylons standing on the dock which sits like a narrow island 100 feet from shore. This is the main gallery, which supports the wide rubber conveyor belts on which grain moves in and out of the elevator. On the inshore side of the dock, on this December morning, barges are being unloaded by means of a pivoting bucket elevator which scoops the grain up and drops it into a covered inclined conveyor rising to the storage bins on shore. A whole string of barges is waiting to be emptied: some hold wheat from Minnesota, others corn from Illinois and Iowa; two of Gus Critz's soybean barges are also here, and their cargo will be mixed with that of other countless barges and railroad cars which have been bringing soybeans to Destrehan since harvest time. Ships are of course loaded from these commingled elevator stocks, and it is thus entirely possible that some of the Osceola soybeans may actually end up in the holds of the *New Haven,* which is just being moored to the offshore side of the dock.

As the vessel is made fast to the bollards, and the hatches are opened, government inspectors board the ship to make sure that the holds are free from dirt and insect infestation, and therefore suitable to carry grain. The inspection finds no unsatisfactory conditions, and loading is allowed to begin. Deep within the basement of the elevator on shore a belt conveyor is set in motion; over the belt, the gates which close the conical bottoms of certain concrete bins full of soybeans are gradually opened, and an endless yellow stream begins to move towards the headhouse. Falling into a "boot pit" at the end of the belt, the soybeans are lifted by a bucket elevator to the scale floor, where they are weighed five tons at a time, and then dropped on another conveyor belt which takes them out over the bridge of the main gallery as far as the transverse ship-loading gallery above the dock. There they fall onto a cross belt which extends the length of the loading gallery, and from there into spouts connected to swiveling booms which hang outside the gallery and reach down into the hatches of the waiting ship below. As the soybeans begin to pile into the holds, stevedores stand at the edge of the hatches and maneuver the spouts so that the stream of grain is evenly distributed to all corners of the hold as it fills. Up in the headhouse a mechanical device continuously scoops a few beans from the soybean stream to obtain a composite sample representative of the entire cargo. At last the ship is full. The samples are taken to be analyzed and graded by the U. S. Department of Agriculture, the first mate of the *New Haven* signs a receipt acknowledging responsibility for the cargo, the hatches are closed and the mooring cables are cast off. Less than twenty-four hours after arriving at Destrehan, the *New Haven* is on its way down the Mississippi to begin its transatlantic journey.

The next day the shipping documents are airmailed to New York, where Bunge's Grain Traffic Department checks them for accuracy and puts them together for presentation to the buyer. There are many documents involved, and they must all be in exact conformity with contractual requirements. Bills of Lading, invoices, certificates of weight and grade, certificates of insurance, copies of the charter party and of the stowage plan, all the papers are finally assembled and sent on their way to Germany. Speed is of the essence, because not only must the documents arrive in Europe well before the goods, but also, for a cargo like this worth more than $2 million, a delay of just a few days means the loss of thousands of dollars in interest on the money tied up in the shipment. There is no delay in this case, however, and less than a week after the *New Haven* has sailed, the documents are presented to the buyer, whose bank in Germany immediately transfers by cable the amount of the invoice to Bunge's account with a New York bank. Title to the soybeans has passed to the German buyer, and Bunge Corporation's contractual obligations have been fulfilled.

Now another member of the Bunge Group enters the picture. As the *New Haven,* after a rough two weeks' trip, reaches the North Sea and the Hook of Holland, she enters the Europoort, as the newest and outermost section of Rotterdam's harbor is called. There, on land literally wrested from the sea by Dutch ingenuity and industriousness, the discharge facility built and operated by a subsidiary of Koninklijke Bunge B.V. is ready to speed the *New Haven's* cargo to its final destination deep into West Germany. The *New Haven,* with a length of 573 feet and a beam of 75, is a relatively small ship compared to the mammoth 250,000-ton tankers which can enter the Europoort, or even to the 100,000 tonners which the Bunge facility is equipped to handle. But she dwarfs the swarm of self-propelled wooden barges which glide in and out of the mooring basins fronting the elevator, most of them flaunting lace curtains on the windows of the captain's family living quarters on the stern, and many of them topped with gaily waving laundry lines. Four hundred feet from shore, the *New Haven* comes to rest against the fenders lining the seven-hundred-foot concrete dock on which two gigantic steel towers straddle a long covered structure housing the wide belt conveyors. Like the trunks of nightmarish pachyderms, four pneumatic suckers swing out from each tower on electronically controlled booms, ready to plunge into the vessel's holds and retrieve its golden cargo.

On shore all arrangements for discharge have been made. The buyer's representative has surrendered the Bills of Lading, and inspectors have been appointed to supervise the unloading of the soybeans carried by the *New Haven.* Ten thousand tons are to be transferred directly to barges for immediate shipment to the buyer's crushing plant, while the balance is to be stored in the concrete silo on shore and shipped later as called for by the buyer's requirements.

The hatches are opened, and the pneumatic suckers are lowered into them. A barge slithers under the inclined gallery which connects the dock to the silo, and ties up on the dock's inshore side. Giant electric motors start up, gears rumble, and an endless stream of soybeans begins to flow up the suckers and into the towers to be weighed. From one tower, soybeans are spouted across into the waiting barge; from the other they fall on the belt which runs the length of the dock, and are conveyed over the gallery to the silo and then elevated and dropped into the concrete storage bins. On and on the discharge progresses, the suckers sinking deeper and deeper into the holds as the lightened vessel rises higher and higher over the waterline. As one barge is filled, another takes its place; stevedores climb down into the *New Haven's* holds to maneuver the suckers into the fast diminishing piles and collect every last bit of the cargo. At midnight work stops, but it is resumed early the next day. By midafternoon the *New Haven* is empty, and it sails in ballast towards Philadelphia where a cargo of corn is awaiting transportation to England. On the eight barges loaded directly from the ship, some of Gus Critz's Arkansas soybeans start on the last leg of their journey.

In single file, the barges navigate on the New Waterway, carved out of the estuary of the Meuse River, through Rotterdam's inner harbor and out of the city. Soon the New Meuse turns into the Lek, another of the maze of rivers and canals which are the mainstay of Holland's transportation system. Near Rijswijk, where almost three centuries earlier the ambassadors of Louis XIV and William of Orange signed the peace which ended King William's War, the Lek flows into the Rhine, the "artery of Europe" on which the barges will remain until they reach Mannheim 350 miles upriver. At dusk the barges sight Emmerich, on the German border, and tie up for the night in a mooring basin. Dawn finds them once more in midstream, pushing against the sluggish current, and for the next five days they will use every daylight hour to extend their southward journey. Passing through the heart of the Ruhr Valley, the barges leave behind Duisburg, Europe's largest inland port, and move past Dusseldorf and Cologne. South of Bonn, they go under the Remagen Bridge, key to the Allied crossing of the Rhine in World War II, and further on pass below the legendary Lorelei rock. Late on the sixth day, the eight barges reach the outskirts of Mannheim and are warped at the dock of the buyer's plant. The next morning the soybeans are discharged into the storage silo, from which they will soon go into the mill and be converted into protein feed and vegetable oil.

From the lush fields of the New World to the humming factories of the Old, another cargo of life-sustaining grain has been moved by the work of an American exporter, and the typical transaction described in these pages could be duplicated *ad infinitum,* whether referring to soybeans or wheat or corn.

Not all transactions run so smoothly, of course, and a few final words describing the functions and expertise of a good grain exporter should be added, lest the reader receive too simplistic a picture of the export grain trade.

A grain exporter bears a large responsibility for the proper marketing of America's farm products, and part of his role is to project the future, since he must formulate and express selling ideas for whatever quantity, grade, or distant position the foreign buyers may want, and do this for grain as well as for ocean freight. This forecasting ability and decisiveness are only acquired after years of training have gone to complement an essentially innate business sense. A good grain exporter, furthermore, must follow and interpret correctly, not only crop forecasts and trade developments, but world news in general, since he must hedge against events which on the surface are far removed from the grain trade, but which in actuality are bound to affect it.

A grain exporter has less choice of timing than almost any other kind of businessman: he must either buy first when the farmer wants to sell, or sell first when the foreign importer wants to buy. And concluding the purchase or the sale is only half the job, for the logistic task which follows is a complicated jigsaw puzzle on whose efficient solution often hangs the difference between loss and profit. Profit which, incidentally, is kept to extremely slim proportions by the acute competitiveness of the international bulk commodity trade.

Narrow trading margins make it imperative for an exporter to rely on large volume to produce financially satisfactory results, and such large volume makes it necessary for the trader to become an expert in hedging in the futures markets in order to limit the risk to the vast sums which must be invested in huge grain stocks.

When he has learned the trade, surmounted the hurdles, and solved the problems, the grain exporter must still face his equals in the marketplace and doggedly compete for the actual business, with scrupulous observance of antitrust legislation and under the watchful eyes of many government agencies.

It is, in summation, hard but fascinating work, requiring highly specialized skills, and providing its practitioners with nerve-wracking tensions but also with the rewarding knowledge that they are performing an essential function of national importance. There is no doubt that the activities of grain exporters continue to be no less vital for the American economy than they were in 1860, when the Superintendent of the U. S. Census wrote:

> The grain merchant has been in all countries, but more particularly in this, the pioneer of commerce, whether we refer to the ocean or to the inland trade, and not till he was established could other commercial adventurers find a foothold. The commercial history of the United States is based mainly on breadstuffs—staples always marketable at some quotation wherever the human family dwells.[4]

Notes To Chapter VIII

1. Exhaustive treatments of the modern grain trade from a technical rather than a historical standpoint are found in A. A. Hooker, *The International Grain Trade* (London: Sir Isaac Pitman & Sons, Ltd., 1939), James S. Schonberg, *The Grain Trade: How It Works* (New York: Exposition Press, 1956), and Carl J. Vosloh, Jr., *Grain Marketing* (Washington, D.C.: U. S. Department of Agriculture, Economic Research Service, 1966).

2. The name, originally Bunge North American Grain Corporation, was changed to Bunge Corporation on August 31, 1943.

3. An interesting account of this company's origins is found in John L. Work, *Cargill Beginnings . . . an Account of Early Years* (Minneapolis: Cargill, Inc., 1965).

4. *Eighth Census of the United States,* 1860, Agriculture, pp. cxxxv-cxxxvi.

Destrehan. Bunge's export elevator at Destrehan, Louisiana.
(Sam Sutton, New Orleans)

Destrehan. A rear view of Bunge's Destrehan elevator, showing
the soybean extraction plant and meal storage shed.
(Sam Sutton, New Orleans)

One aspect of grain testing: Using a divider for separating grain sample into representative portions.
(United States Department of Agriculture)

Using hand sieves, removing some weed seeds which function as dockage.
(United States Department of Agriculture)

The inspector makes several operations sometimes required in grading wheat. A small portion of the representative sample is carefully weighed and analyzed to determine the percent of different classes of wheat, damaged kernels, and such other grading factors as may be necessary.

(United States Department of Agriculture)

Using a moisture meter to determine the moisture content of a sample of grain sent for testing to the Kansas City, Missouri Office of the Agricultural Marketing Service of the United States Department of Agriculture.

(United States Department of Agriculture)

The *Quebec*, a modern bulk carrier of about 50,000 tons.

Europoort Silo, N. V.—Completed in 1972, this modern facility includes storage for 100,000 tons of grain and is equipped to discharge vessels at a speed of 2,000 tons an hour.

(KLM Aerocarto N. V.)

Europoort Silo, N. V.—While a large ocean-going vessel is being discharged pneumatically, grain is transferred to the holds of two North Sea coasters. Simultaneously, grain from the storage silo is loaded on barges moored under the gallery which connects the dock to the silo.

(Panavue, Rotterdam)

Europoort Silo, N. V.—A closeup of the pneumatic discharge towers.

(Panavue, Rotterdam)

Wheat is unloaded in the port of Goa, India, in January, 1966. Wheat is unloaded from a ship into boxcars. Sacks are then filled from spouts of boxcars.
(United States Department of Agriculture)

U. S. Wheat, newly arrived in Bombay, India, May 1959.
(United States Department of Agriculture)

U. S. wheat, supplied under the Food for Peace (PL480) program, being unloaded at a port in Pakistan.
(United States Department of Agriculture)

A happy young cultivator hugs a few stalks of wheat in a field near the village of Varanasi. Uttar Pradesh, India.
(United States Department of Agriculture)

With India working to expand its own grain production, and with wheat from the U. S. (sold to India under Public Law 480) coming into Indian ports at the rate of at least a shipload a day, grain storage facilities had to be expanded. This modern 10,000 ton grain storage facility was completed and put into use in 1959 at Hapur, Uttar Pradesh. The U. S. gave some financial assistance to the construction, using rupees from PL480 sales.
(United States Department of Agriculture)

This is a warehouse at a grain elevator in Calcutta, built in 1966 by Agency for International Development funds.
(United States Department of Agriculture)

U. S. bagged grain being moved from ship to truck for transporting to the Eritrean highlands of Ethiopia, where drought and locusts severely damaged harvests in 1963.

American food and feed being unloaded at a port in Jordan in
1963. Food aid from the United States—shipped under PL480—
has gone to 116 countries since the program was launched in
1954.

(United States Department of Agriculture)

Bibliography

Baer, Julius B. and Olin Glenn Saxon. *Commodity Exchanges and Futures Trading.* New York: Harper & Brothers, Publishers, 1949.

Baker, Gladys L., Wayne D. Rasmussen, Vivian Wiser, and Jane M. Porter. *Century of Service: The First 100 Years of the Department of Agriculture.* Washington, D.C.: Government Printing Office, 1963.

Bell, Richard E. "U. S. Wheat Sales to Japan—A Payoff for U. S. Market Development." *Foreign Agriculture,* Vol. IX, No. 16 (April 19, 1971).

Benedict, Murray R. *Can We Solve the Farm Problem, An Analysis of Federal Aid to Agriculture.* New York: The Twentieth Century Fund, 1955.

——————————————. *Farm Policies of the United States, 1790-1950.* New York: The Twentieth Century Fund, 1953.

—————————————— and Oscar C. Stine. *The Agricultural Commodity Programs—Two Decades of Experience.* New York: The Twentieth Century Fund, 1956.

Benson, Ezra Taft. *Freedom to Farm.* Garden City, N. Y.: Doubleday & Company, 1960.

Bezanson, Anne, Robert D. Gray, and Miriam Hussey. *Prices in Colonial Pennsylvania.* Philadelphia: University of Pennsylvania Press, 1935.

Bidwell, Percy Wells and John I. Falconer, *History of Agriculture in the Northern United States 1620-1860.* New York: Peter Smith, 1941.

Bjork, Gordon C. "The Weaning of the American Economy: Independence, Market Changes, and Economic Development." *The Journal of Economic History,* Vol. XXIV, No. 4 (December, 1964).

Bradford, William. *History of Plymouth Plantation.* Edited by W. T. Davis. New York: C. Scribner's Sons, 1908.

Brunchey, Stuart. *The Roots of American Economic Growth, 1607-1861: An Essay in Social Causation.* London: Hutchinson & Co., Ltd., 1965.

Brunthaver, Carroll G. "Agricultural Act of 1970: Its Trade Implications." *Foreign Agriculture,* Vol. VIII, No. 49 (December 7, 1970).

Checkland, S. G. "American Versus West Indian Traders in Liverpool, 1793-1815." *The Journal of Economic History,* Vol. XVIII, No. 2 (June 1958).

Christenson, Reo M. *The Brannan Plan—Farm Politics and Policy.* Ann Arbor: University of Michigan Press, 1959.

Chumley, G. N. "Postwar Shifts in U. S. Agricultural Export Trade." *Foreign Agriculture,* Vol XIII, No. 11 (November, 1949).

Clark, John G. *The Grain Trade in the Old Northwest.* Urbana and London: University of Illinois Press, 1966.

Commission on International Trade and Investment Policy. *United States International Economic Policy in an Interdependent World.* Washington, D. C.: U. S. Government Printing Office, 1971.

Coppock, John O. *North Atlantic Policy—The Agricultural Gap.* New York: The Twentieth Century Fund, 1963.

Dam, Kenneth W. *The GATT Law and International Economic Organization.* Chicago and London: The University of Chicago Press, 1970.

Dart, Joseph. "The Grain Elevators of Buffalo." *Buffalo Historical Society Publications,* I (1879).

Dean, John Ward, Editor. *Capt. John Mason.* Boston: The Prince society, 1887.

deCastro, Josue. *The Geography of Hunger.* Boston: Little, Brown and Company, 1952.

Edwards, Everett E. "American Agriculture—The First 300 Years." *Yearbook of Agriculture—1940.* 76th Congress, 3rd Session— House Document No. 695.

Evans, Charles H. "Exports, Domestic and Foreign from the American Colonies to Great Britain, from 1697 to 1789, Inclusive. Exports, Domestic and Foreign from the United States to All Countries, from 1789 to 1883, Inclusive." *House Miscellaneous Documents,* 48 Cong. 1 Sess. No. 49, Part 2 (1884), Serial 7236.

Fite, Gilbert C. *American Agriculture and Farm Policy Since 1900.* New York: The Macmillan Company, 1964.

——————————————————. *George N. Peek and the Fight for Farm Parity.* Norman: University of Oklahoma Press, 1954.

Food and Agriculture Organization of the United Nations. *Development Through Food: A Strategy for Surplus Utilization.* Rome: FAO, 1961.

——————————————————. *The State of Food and Agriculture 1965: Review of the Second Postwar Decade.* Rome: FAO, 1965.

Galpin, W. Freeman. *The Grain Supply of England During the Napoleonic Period.* New York: The Macmillan Company, 1925.

Gates, Paul W. *Agriculture and the Civil War.* New York: Alfred A. Knopf, 1965.

Ginzberg, Eli. "The Economics of British Neutrality during the Civil War." *Agricultural History,* Vol 10 (October, 1936).

Gras, Norman Scott Brien. *A History of Agriculture in Europe and America.* New York: F. S. Crofts & Co., Publishers, 1925.

———————————————. *The Evolution of the English Corn Market.* Cambridge: Harvard University Press, 1915.

Hall, Tom Gibson, Jr. *Cheap Bread from Dear Wheat: Herbert Hoover, the Wilson Administration, and the Management of Wheat Prices, 1916-1920.* Unpublished Doctoral Dissertation University of California, Davis, 1968.

Hanna, Mary A. *The Trade of the Delaware District before the Revolution.* Northampton, Mass.: Dept. of History of Smith College, 1917.

Hoffman, Paul G. *World Without Want.* New York: Harper & Row, 1962.

Jameson, J. Franklin, Editor. *Johnson's Wonder Working Providence, 1628-1651.* New York: C. Scribner's Sons, 1910.

Johnson, Emory R., T. W. Van Metre, G. G. Huebner, and D. S. Hanchett, *History of Domestic and Foreign Commerce of the United States.* Washington, D.C.: The Carnegie Institution of Washington, 1915.

Jones, Robert H. "Long Live the King?". *Agricultural History,* Vol. 37, No. 3 (July, 1963).

Kuhlmann, Charles B. *The Development of the Flour Milling Industry in the United States.* Boston and New York: Houghton Mifflin Company, 1929.

Leclerc, J. A. *International Trade in Wheat and Wheat Flour.* Washington, D.C.: U. S. Government Printing Office, 1925.

Lee, Guy A. "The Historical Significance of the Chicago Grain Elevator System." *Agricultural History,* Vol. 11, No. 1 (January, 1937).

Lydon, James G. "Fish and Flour for Gold: Southern Europe and the Colonial American Balance of Payments." *Business History Review,* Vol. XXXIX, No. 2 (Summer 1965).

Malenbaum, Wilfred. *The World Wheat Economy, 1885-1939.* Cambridge: Harvard University Press, 1953.

Martin, Thomas P. "The Staff of Life in Diplomacy and Politics during the Early Eighteen-Fifties." *Agricultural History,* Vol. 18, No. 1 (January 1944).

McGovern, George, Editor. *Agricultural Thought in the Twentieth Century.* Indianapolis and New York: The Bobbs-Merrill Company, Inc., 1967.

———————————————. *War Against Want: America's Food For Peace Program.* New York: Walker and Company, 1964.

Merk, Frederick. "The British Corn Crisis of 1845-46 And The Oregon Treaty." *Agricultural History,* Vol. 8, No. 3 (July, 1934).

"Monthly Summary of Foreign Commerce." Washington, D.C., Bureau of Foreign and Domestic Commerce, 1880-1900.

Morris, Richard B., Editor. *Encyclopedia of American History.* New York: Harper & Row, Publishers, 1965.

National Advisory Commission on Food and Fiber. *Foreign Trade and Agricultural Policy.* Washington, D.C.: U. S. Government Printing Office, 1967.

Nettels, Curtis P. "British Mercantilism and the Economic Development of the Thirteen Colonies." *The Journal of Economic History,* Vol. XII, No. 2 (Spring 1952).

——————————. *The Roots of American Civilization: A History of American Colonial Life.* 2nd ed. New York: Appleton Century-Crofts, 1963.

Norris, Frank. *The Pit.* New York: Grove Press, Inc., 1956.

North, Douglass C. *The Economic Growth of the United States, 1790-1860.* Englewood Cliffs, N.J.: Prentice-Hall, Inc., 1961.

Odle, Thomas D. "The American Grain Trade of the Great Lakes, 1825-1873." *Inland Seas,* VII (1952).

Ostrander, Gilman M. "The Colonial Molasses Trade." *Agricultural History,* Vol. 30, No. 2 (April 1956).

Palmby, Clarence D. "The World Feed Situation in the 1970's." *Foreign Agriculture,* Vol. VII, No. 24 (June 16, 1969).

——————————. "Changes Shaping World Feedgrain Trade." *Foreign Agriculture,* Vol. VIII, No. 5 (February 2, 1970).

Peek, George N. and Hugh S. Johnson. *Equality for Agriculture,* 2nd Ed. Moline, Ill.: Moline Plow Company, 1922.

Perkins, Van L. *Crisis in Agriculture: The Agricultural Adjustment Administration and the New Deal, 1933.* Berkeley and Los Angeles: University of California Press, 1969.

Pitkin, Timothy. *A Statistical View of the Commerce of the United States of America.* New Haven: Durrie & Peck, 1835.

President's Science Advisory Committee. *The World Food Problem.* Washington, D.C.: U. S. Government Printing Office, 1967.

Price, H. Bruce. "Grain Standardization." *American Economic Review,* II (June, 1921).

Rahe, Dewain H. and Isaac E. Lemon. "The First Billion Dollar Customer." *Foreign Agriculture,* Vol. VIII, No. 35 (August 31, 1970).

Rasmussen, Wayne D., Editor. *Readings in the History of American Agriculture.* Urbana: University of Illinois Press, 1960.

——————————. "Forty Years of Agricultural History." *Agricultural History,* Vol. 33, No. 4 (October 1959).

Report of the Federal Trade Commission on Methods and Opera-

tions of Grain Exporters. Washington, D.C.: Government Printing Office, 1922-3.

Riddell, William Renwick. "Suggested Governmental Assistance to Farmers Two Centuries Ago, in Pennsylvania." *Pennsylvania Magazine of History and Biography,* LIII (1929).

Rothstein, Morton. *American Wheat and the British Market, 1860-1905.* Unpublished doctoral dissertation, Cornell University, 1960.

Sachs, William S. "Agricultural Conditions in the Northern Colonies Before the Revolution." *The Journal of Economic History,* Vol. XIII, No. 3 (Summer 1953).

Saloutos, Theodore and John D. Hicks. *Agricultural Discontent in the Middle West, 1900-1939.* Madison: University of Wisconsin Press, 1951.

Schlebecker, John T. "The World Metropolis and the History of American Agriculture." *The Journal of Economic History,* Vol. XX, No. 2 (June 1960).

Schmidt, Louis Bernard. "The Influence of Wheat and Cotton on Anglo-American Relations during the Civil War." *Iowa Journal of History and Politics,* XVI (July 1918).

Shepherd, James F. "Commodity Exports from the British North American Colonies to Overseas Areas, 1768-1772: Magnitudes and Patterns of Trade." *Explorations In Economic History,* Vol. 8, No. 1 Fall 1970.

Shideler, James H. *Farm Crisis 1919-1923.* Berkeley and Los Angeles: University of California Press, 1957.

Statistical Abstract of the United States. Washington, D.C.: U. S. Department of Commerce, 1947, 1948.

Sterns, Worthy P. "The Foreign Trade of the United States from 1820 to 1840." *The Journal of Political Economy,* VIII (December 1899).

Surface, Frank M. and Raymond L. Bland. *American Food in the World War and Reconstruction Period.* Palo Alto: Stanford University Press, 1931.

―――――――――――――――. *The Grain Trade During the World War.* New York: Macmillan Company, 1928.

Taylor, George Rogers. "American Economic Growth Before 1840: An Exploratory Essay." *The Journal of Economic History,* XXIV, No. 4 (December 1964).

"The Grain Trade of the United States." *Monthly Summary of Commerce and Finance.* Washington, D.C.: United States Treasury Department, Bureau of Statistics, January, 1900.

Thomasson, Larry F. "The Story of the 1960's: U. S. Feed Grains in World Trade." *Foreign Agriculture,* Vol. III, No. 3 (January 19, 1970).

Tinbergen, Jan. *Shaping the World Economy.* New York: The Twentieth Century Fund, 1962.

Toma, Peter A. *The Politics of Food for Peace.* Tucson: The University of Arizona Press, 1967.

Trollope, Anthony. *North America.* London: 1862.

United States Department of Agriculture. *Agricultural Statistics.* Washington, D.C.: United States Printing Office, 1967, 1970, 1971.

——————————————, *Compilation of Statutes.* Washington, D.C.: U. S. Government Printing Office, 1969.

Wallace, Henry A. *The American Choice.* New York: Reynal and Hitchcock, 1940.

Walton, Gary M. "New Evidence on Colonial Commerce." *Journal of Economic History,* XXVIII, No. 3 (Sept. 1968).

Weeden, W. B. *Social and Economic History of New England 1620-1789.* Boston and New York: Houghton, Mifflin and Company, 1890.

Wilcox, Walter W. *The Farmer and the Second World War.* Ames: Iowa State College Press, 1947.

Winthrop, John. *Winthrop's Journal.* "History of New England," 1630-1649, Edited by James K. Hosmer. New York: C. Scribner's Sons, 1908, II.

Wunderlich, Herbert J. "Foreign Grain Trade of the United States 1835-1860." *Journal of History and Politics,* Vol. XXXIII (January 1935).

Index